ADVANCE PRAISE FOR *THE COMPLETE GEEZER GUIDEBOOK*

"I predict *The Complete Geezer Guidebook* will be a runaway best seller."
—Nostradamus

"If I'd read *Geezer* a little earlier, there'd be a couple of more commandments!"
—Moses

"I've never been so insulted in my life! Off with a few heads!"
—Henry VIII

"Any geezer who has been good this year will find the *The Complete Geezer Guidebook* book under his tree."
—Santa Claus

THE COMPLETE GEEZER GUIDEBOOK

THE COMPLETE
GEEZER
GUIDEBOOK

EVERYTHING YOU NEED TO KNOW
ABOUT BEING OLD AND GRUMPY!

— • —

Charles F. "Chuck" Adams

Quill Driver Books
Fresno, CA

The Complete Geezer Guidebook
© 2009 Charles F. Adams. All rights reserved.

Published by Quill Driver Books,
an imprint of Linden Publishing.
2006 S. Mary, Fresno, California, 93721
559-233-6633 / 800-345-4447
QuillDriverBooks.com

Quill Driver Books and Colophon are trademarks of
Linden Publishing, Inc.

Quill Driver Books project cadre:
Carla Green, Stephen Blake Mettee, Kent Sorsky

ISBN: 978-1-884956-98-0 (1-884956-98-X)

35798642

Printed in the USA on acid-free paper.

Library of Congress Cataloging-in-Publication Data

Adams, Charles F.
  The complete geezer guidebook : everything you need to know
about being old and grumpy! / by Charles F. Adams.
      p. cm.
  Includes bibliographical references.
  ISBN 978-1-884956-98-0 (pbk. : acid-free paper)
  1. Aging—Humor. 2. Old age—Humor. 3. Older people—Humor.
I. Title.
  PN6231.A43A66 2009
  818'.607—dc22
                                      2009028015

This book is dedicated to geezers the world over—
to those gentlemen whose longevity, crankiness, and
eccentric natures have endeared them to their families,
their friends, and their communities. May they all live long
and lustily—and may they all buy and read this book to
attain a fuller understanding of their role in society
and their place in the world order.

C.F.A.
(a geezer)

This book is also dedicated to the legendary cartoonists of *The New Yorker*—whose works enliven these pages and make reading this book bearable.

Peter Arno	Warren Miller
Bruce Bairnsfather	Frank Modell
Charles Barsotti	Michael Muslin
George Booth	W.B. Park
Leo Callum	George Price
Roz Chast	Mischa Richter
Tom Cheney	Al Ross
Frank Cotham	Brian Savage
Whitney Darrow, Jr.	Charles Saxon
Eldon Didini	David Sipress
J.C. Duffy	Barbara Smallor
Mort Gerberg	Mick Stevens
Herbert Goldberg	Richard Taylor
J.B. Handelsman	Mike Twohy
Zachary Kanin	P.C. Vey
Edward Koren	Robert Weber
Robert Kraus	Gluyas Williams
Eric Lewis	Graham Wilson
Lee Lorenz	

With illustrations by Clark Tate ...
and with thanks to Merredith Miller of the Cartoon Bank.

CONTENTS

INTRODUCTION

If you have just purchased this book, there must be a reason. That is, unless you thought you were buying *another* book and picked this one up by accident, in which case you should go to the bookstore and get your money back.

But let's assume for the moment that you knew what you were doing. This means that you either suspect that you are a geezer yourself, or you are about to become a geezer, or you know someone who is or has recently become a geezer. There is no chance that you used to be a geezer—because once you have attained geezerhood, there is no going back—no retreat—not even any diminishment. Once a geezer, always a geezer! In short, the only former geezer is a dead geezer!

A DEFINITION

geezer—(gē - zər) n. Slang. An eccentric, grumpy old man.

[Probably a dialectical pronunciation of *guiser*, or one in disguise. Also from the Middle English *giser*, meaning to masquerade. Or possibly from the Latin *gesarius*, meaning a mature fletus; or, in the vernacular, an old fart.]

"*Thank God! A panel of experts!*"

CHAPTER ONE

ARE YOU A GEEZER?
(The Following Pages Will Give You the Answer)

HOW DO YOU KNOW
IF YOU ARE A GEEZER?

SOME OF THE evidence is already in. You are, after all, reading this book. That means that you are at least pondering the possibility. Or perhaps someone gave you this book—which at least means that they believed the gift was appropriate.

So it's time to take the next step—and examine your true geezer potential.

LET'S BEGIN THE JOURNEY

HURDLE #1—ARE YOU A MAN?

The first requirement is that you must be male. There is no such thing as a female geezer. The possibility of such a thing has been raised time and again, and the answer has always been in the negative. Dictionary after dictionary has made this clear over the decades. However, since the concept of the female geezer seems to linger on and persist in the writings of some avant-garde feminist writers, a panel of experts was convened in July of 1998 in Zurich, Switzerland, to consider all aspects of this question. Their verdict, issued in a paper entitled "Geezers and the Sexual Component," has brought the issue to a definite close. Their finding: Any female with geezer characteristics cannot be considered a "geezer." She is, instead, "an old biddy."

"You have <u>so</u> got it turned off!"

HURDLE #2—ARE YOU AN OLD FART?

It is important at this point to draw a distinction between "old farts" and "geezers," for they are not always the same thing. It is relatively easy, for instance, to become an old fart. All you have to do is have the courage and patience to endure the passage of time. Rich or poor, loved or hated, sane or demented, you will automatically become an old fart if you can just manage to hang around long enough.

But age alone will not earn you the title of "geezer." To be a true geezer, a man must have, in addition to age, a certain attitude, disposition, frame of mind, and outlook on life that not all old farts can achieve.

To put it another way, all geezers may be old farts, but not all old farts are geezers. For instance, no one could deny that Methuselah was an old fart. The Bible says that he lived to be 969 years old, which may, in fact, make him the oldest old fart in history. Yet there is no evidence that he was not of

"Wunderkinder come and go, but old farts are forever."

even disposition, unfailing good spirits, and tolerant toward his fellow man. In other words, *not* a geezer!

Moses, on the other hand, not only lived to a great age, but apparently pissed off a lot of people along the way—with his constant preaching and haranguing the feint-of-heart—and demanding that everyone follow him into a new land. And let's not forget his coming up with those ten commandments—perhaps the grumpiest act of all time! In other words, it's pretty safe to say that Moses was both an old fart *and* a geezer!

So next, we must determine quantitatively and qualitatively, whether or not *you* are an "old fart."

To find the answer, you should take the following test. It is not difficult, and will require a minimum of time and effort. Simply answer "yes" or "no" to the following questions—and be sure to keep track of your total responses as you go.

READY, GET SET, GO!

THE "OLD FART" TEST

Do you remember, from your own personal experience, any of the following:

1. When you didn't have to look for the car keys because you always kept them in the car.
   YES ___ **NO** ___

2. When there were wire "rabbit" ears on top of the television.
   YES ___ **NO** ___

3. When no kid had any idea what breed his dog was.
   YES ___ **NO** ___

4. When milk came in glass bottles and the cream was all at the top.
   YES ___ **NO** ___

5. When the Fuller Brush Man came to your house at least once a year.
   YES ___ **NO** ___

6. When a gallon of gasoline cost 25 cents and a gas station attendant pumped it for you.
   YES ___ **NO** ___

7. When a dollar once a week was considered a fine allowance.
   YES ___ **NO** ___

8. When you would stop to pick up a penny.
   YES ___ **NO** ___

9. When "kick the can" was considered a really exciting game.
   YES ___ **NO** ___

10. When being spanked by mom or dad couldn't get them arrested.
    YES ___ **NO** ___

11. When telephone numbers started with a name or word.
    YES ___ **NO** ___

12. When coloring books, Lincoln Logs and Tinkertoys were considered wonderful Christmas presents.
    YES ___ **NO** ___

13. When there weren't any stores called McDonalds or Starbucks or Costco.
    YES ___ **NO** ___

14. When you went to the movies and saw a double feature and the newsreel.
    YES ___ **NO** ___

15. When you got Green Stamps with your groceries.
    YES ___ **NO** ___

16. When there was a handle on the ice tray that you pulled to loosen the cubes.
    YES ___ **NO** ___

17. When things you bought at the drug store weren't hermetically sealed or had "adult proof" safety caps.
    YES ___ **NO** ___

18. How weird the glass looked after you drank the buttermilk.
    YES ___ **NO** ___

19. When typewriters made a clacking noise and you had to use carbon paper to get copies.
    YES ___ **NO** ___

20. When you thought the worst thing you could get from a girl was "cooties."
YES ___ **NO** ___

21. When everybody supported the country when it went to war.
YES ___ **NO** ___

22. When there weren't any adults hanging around when you played baseball with your friends.
YES ___ **NO** ___

23. When you could send a letter by "Special Delivery" or "Air Mail," and the postman came twice every day.
YES ___ **NO** ___

24. When drugstores had things called soda fountains.
YES ___ **NO** ___

25. When kids came home from school and their mothers were there to greet them.
YES ___ **NO** ___

26. Can you identify a majority of the following (answers on the following page—no peeking):

a. Mercurochrome	**YES** ___	**NO** ___
b. A slide rule	**YES** ___	**NO** ___
c. BVD's	**YES** ___	**NO** ___
d. Moola	**YES** ___	**NO** ___
e. A rumble seat	**YES** ___	**NO** ___
f. A davenport	**YES** ___	**NO** ___
g. An ice box	**YES** ___	**NO** ___
h. Dr. Denton's	**YES** ___	**NO** ___
i. The Palmer Method	**YES** ___	**NO** ___
j. A flick	**YES** ___	**NO** ___
k. Braces	**YES** ___	**NO** ___
l. The cellar	**YES** ___	**NO** ___

Answers to #26
   a. You put it on small cuts and scrapes
   b. Engineering students wore them hanging from their belts
   c. One-piece underwear
   d. Money
   e. A seat for two that opened up over the trunk of the car
   f. A large couch
   g. A refrigerator
   h. Pajamas with legs, feet, and a flap in the back
   i. Cursive handwriting
   j. A movie
   k. Suspenders to hold your pants up
   l. The basement

Now the time has come to add up the total number of "yes" answers. If you answered at least twenty of the questions in the affirmative, then you are most assuredly an "old fart." Congratulations!

If you are not an "old fart," you should probably discontinue reading this book—and give it to someone who is older and wiser. But if you *did* pass, you need to continue with the remainder of this examination—because now the question is...

MOVIE STARS ONLY OLD FARTS REMEMBER
Edward G. Robinson
Gloria Swanson
Hedy Lamar
Abbot and Costello
Glenn Ford
Gene Tierney
Dick Powell
Carmen Miranda
Norma Shearer
George Brent
Ann Sheridan
Myrna Loy
Sonny Tufts
Pat O'Brien
Paulette Goddard

WHEN DOES AN OLD FART CROSS OVER INTO TRUE GEEZERHOOD?

HURDLE #3—ARE YOU A GEEZER?

True geezers have a mind-set, an attitude toward life that clearly distinguishes them from ordinary, run-of-the-mill people. The following test is designed both to reconfirm your status as an old fart and to let you know if you have the "right stuff" to make your own claim to geezerhood.

GOOD LUCK!

THE GREAT GEEZER TEST

(Circle the number which best describes your likely attitude or response.)

When you are presented with a birthday cake with lots of candles on it:
1. You are grateful to be starting yet another of your "golden years."
2. You hate the fact that you are a year older.
3. You don't give a damn how old you are.
4. You wonder why the cake is on fire.

When you see a photo of yourself taken forty years ago:
1. You're surprised how little you've changed.
2. You're horrified at how much you've changed.
3. You don't give a damn how much you've changed.
4. You don't recognize yourself.

When your eye doctor asks you to read the chart on the wall:
1. You read it carefully.
2. You can't see the letters.
3. You can't see the chart.
4. You can't see the wall.

When you settle down for a much needed night's sleep and the neighbor's dog starts barking:
1. You try to catnap in between dog barks.
2. You call the neighbor about the dog.
3. You call the police, the fire department and the SPCA about the dog.
4. You get a good night's sleep because you are stone deaf.

When your family tells you it's time for you to stop driving, it will be because:

1. You drive too fast.
2. You drive too slow.
3. You tend to run into things.
4. You often park in someone else's garage.

THE THREE STAGES OF GEEZER FORGETFULNESS

1. Forgetting names.
2. Forgetting to zip up.
3. Forgetting to zip down!

If a friend were to give you a book entitled *How to Improve Your Memory:*

1. You would accept it gratefully, saying you hope it will help you remember things.
2. You would accept the book, but be secretly hurt by its implications.
3. You would give the book back and tell your friend that he should read the damn thing himself.
4. You would intend to read the book, but wouldn't be able to remember where you put it.

If you ever receive a notice that your driver's license has been suspended you would:

1. Accept it graciously, thinking it was all for the best.
2. Try to find out immediately how to appeal the suspension.
3. Call your lawyer to start a lawsuit against the State.
4. Be surprised to learn that you still *had* a driver's license.

You take fewer walks these days because:

1. You have a sore knee.
2. You have two sore knees.
3. You have two sore knees and a sore hip.
4. You keep getting lost.

When your doctor tells you that you should cut down on your drinking:
1. You are grateful for the advice.
2. You say you'll try but know you'll fail.
3. You ask him how much *he* is drinking these days.
4. You wonder who the man in the white coat is.

If you're on a trip and you become lost:
1. You ask the first person you see for directions.
2. You refuse under any circumstances to ask for directions.
3. You blame your wife for getting you lost.
4. It's not clear to you that you *are* lost.

If you are in a restaurant enjoying dinner and a baby starts crying.
1. You try to enjoy your dinner assuming the mother is doing her best.
2. You demand that the manager do something about the kid.
3. You yell at the mother to make her kid shut the hell up.
4. You think it's your wife and tell her to be quiet.

A big yellow truck suddenly pulls into the lane in front of you and cuts you off.
1. You assume the driver is late for an appointment and you hope he gets there on time.
2. You mutter under your breath and forget about it.
3. You roll down the window, hurl a string of oaths at the driver and give him the finger.
4. You're surprised to find a big yellow truck ahead of you and wonder how he got there.

The next time you attend a 50th celebration, it will probably be:
1.   Your high school reunion.
2.   Your college reunion.
3.   Your son's birthday.
4.   The golden anniversary of your fourth marriage.

WHEN IS A GEEZER NOT A GEEZER?

When he is "Geezer" Butler, bassist for the group called "Black Sabbath." Butler is only 58 years old. Not only is Butler not a real geezer, but he is not even an old fart!!

If you turn on the car radio and find yourself listening to "rap" music:
1.   You listen intently to learn what the younger generation is saying.
2.   You change the station as quickly as possible.
3.   You start yelling obscenities back at the radio.
4.   You wonder when your ex-wife got a recording contract.

You arrive home at night only to find your wife has locked you out:
1.   You spend the rest of the night apologizing and begging to be let in.
2.   You get yourself to the nearest hotel and check in for the night.
3.   You smash your way in through the window, proclaiming that no one is going to keep you out of *your* house.
4.   You assume you got the wrong house and go up and down the block ringing doorbells.

Now add up your total points (between 15 and 60).

If your total is between 15 and 30, you are absolutely *not* a geezer. You are not sufficiently eccentric or crotchety to make the grade. You should probably start reading some other book—maybe *How to Win Friends and Influence People.*

"Intransigent enough for you, sir?"

If your total is between 50 and 60, you are also *not* a geezer. You are, in fact, a *fossil!* It is amazing that you were able to take this test. Pack it in!

BOB HOPE'S OBSERVATIONS AS AN AGING GEEZER:

At Seventy:
"I still chase women, but only downhill."

At Eighty:
"I notice that my birthday suit also needs pressing."

At Ninety:
"My candles now cost more than my cake."

At One Hundred:
"I don't feel old. In fact, I don't feel anything until noon. Then it's time for my nap."

If your total is between 30 and 50, you are definite geezer material. Congratulations! Keep reading this book to fulfill your destiny.

For a more precise appraisal of your status as a geezer or non-geezer, please consult the scientifically calibrated "geez-o-meter" shown on the following page.

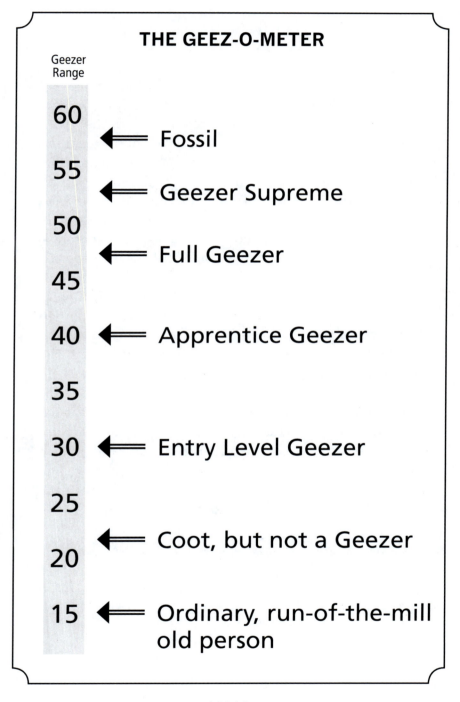

THE GEEZ-O-METER

Geezer
Range

60
⬅ Fossil

55
⬅ Geezer Supreme

50
⬅ Full Geezer

45

40 ⬅ Apprentice Geezer

35

30 ⬅ Entry Level Geezer

25

⬅ Coot, but not a Geezer
20

15 ⬅ Ordinary, run-of-the-mill
old person

THE ACTUAL HISTORY OF THE WORD

The first known use of anything like "geezer" occurred in 1766. In that year, *Sewell and Boys Complete Dictionary of English and Dutch* included the word "geyzer" and defined it as a masculine noun meaning "a foolish old person." Then we skip all the way to 1885 to a book called *The Truth About the Stage,* which on page 16 stated, "If we wake up the old geyser, we shall have to pay full compensation." Fourteen years later, in 1897, *The Westminster Gazette* included this sentence, "So an obliging firm of Liverpool solicitors, like the old geeser in the song." (What song, we don't know, but this implies an earlier song about "geesers.") Then, finally, in 1914, in something called *Dialect Notes IV,* published in Philadelphia, we finally see the word we know and revere today. On page 201 we find this sentence: "The old geezer wouldn't let us play ball in the pasture."

How wonderful! The first time "geezer" actually appears in print, it is used to describe some old farmer who wouldn't let kids play ball in his field. Picture him now—waving his hoe or his pitchfork, railing at a bunch of kids who are trying to have a good time, and threatening to throw them off his property. That's the "geezer" we know and love today!

"Professor Merton is a brilliant man in his field, but he has absolutely no small talk."

CHAPTER TWO

GEEZER TYPES
(Not All Geezers Are Created Equal)

G EEZERS COME IN a wide variety of forms and styles. In fact, the number of identifiable sub-species is too numerous to enumerate in this slender volume. On the following pages, however, are portrayed and described some of the more outstanding and prevalent geezer types. Each is noteworthy for its peculiar habits, appearance and interests. Together, they comprise a vivid cross-section of the *humanis gezarius* currently under examination.

The odds are that you can find your geezer type on one of the following pages.

THE GOLFING GEEZER
(gezarius clubitis)

Found on or near large, open green areas of land. At home has all television sets turned to the Golf Channel. **Subscribes to**: *Golf Magazine, Golf Digest* and *Senior Golf*. **His most prized possession**: His collection of eighty-seven putters, none of which works properly. **Secret desire**: To shoot a score so low he doesn't have to lie about it. **His strongest belief**: That a well-struck four-iron is better than sex.

THE GARDENING GEEZER
(gezarius floribundus)
Found in small patches of cultivated soil. Recognizable by his filthy boots, worn knee patches, and dirty fingernails. **Subscribes to**: *The English Garden* and *Gardener's Monthly*. **Most prized possession**: His dilapidated potting shed. **His greatest fear**: Aphids! **His strongest belief**: That the smell of fertilizer is better than sex.

THE GOURMET GEEZER
(gezarius appetitus)

Frequently found in kitchen areas or hovering near restaurants. Identifiable by his stained tie and his oversized waist. ***Subscribes to****: Gourmet, Bon Appetite,* and *Savoir.* ***Most prized possession****:* His massive collection of cookbooks and menus. ***His greatest fear****:* Discovery that he can't really tell one wine from another. ***His strongest belief****:* That a well-made soufflé is better than sex.

THE HYPOCHONDRIAC GEEZER
(gezarius maladius)

Identifiable by his eagerness to recite his various ailments and recount his numerous surgeries. **Subscribes to**: *The Harvard Health Letter, Wellness Magazine, The Mayo Clinic News*. **Most prized possession**: His cabinet full of more than a hundred prescriptions. **His greatest fear**: That someone will discover he is actually in good health. **Strongest belief**: That a visit to the doctor is better than sex.

THE PROFESSORIAL GEEZER
(gezarius intellectualis)

Found mostly in and near university towns. Identifiable by his rimless glasses and his bad haircut. **Subscribes to**: *Atlantic Monthly*, *The Harvard Review*, and *The Economist*. **Most prized possession**: The numerous framed degrees that hang in his office. **His greatest fear**: Discovery that he is unpublished. **His strongest belief**: That a well-delivered lecture is better than sex.

THE FISHING GEEZER
(gezarius pescatoris)
Found mostly in lakes, rivers, and swampy areas. Is convinced that it is worth spending a thousand dollars on equipment to catch ten dollars' worth of fish. **Subscribes to**: *Field and Stream* and *American Angler*. **Most prized possession**: His collection of 287 trout flies, few of which have landed a fish. **His strongest belief**: That a hard strike in a fast-moving stream is better than sex.

THE "NEST EGG" GEEZER
(gezarius miserus)

Can usually be found at his computer where he watches over and tries to enhance his IRA, his SEP-IRA and his ROTH. **Subscribes to**: *Wall Street Journal, Forbes, Money* and *Barrons*. **Proudest accomplishment**: Buying Microsoft at 21. **Greatest fear**: Going broke. **Strongest belief**: That watching the Dow Jones go up is better than sex.

THE BIRD-WATCHING GEEZER
(gezarius ornitholis)

Can frequently be spotted behind bushes or hiding in back of trees. Identifiable by the upward tilt of his head and the squint of his eyes. **Subscribes to**: *Bird Times, Birder's World* and *Birds and Blooms*. **Proudest accomplishment**: Being the first in his club to own both a hand-held bird-identifying computer and a Sierra Z56 Night Monocular. **Strongest belief**: That spotting spring's first robin is better than sex.

THE VAGABOND GEEZER
(gezarius wanderius)

Left over from the 1960s—a residue of the hippie generation. Identifiable by his unkempt beard, ragged clothing and an ever-present guitar slung over his shoulder. Nomadic by nature, difficult to track. **Most prized possession**: His fabricated memories of being at Woodstock. **Greatest fear**: Discovery that he can't actually play the guitar. **Strongest belief**: That hearing a song by the Grateful Dead is better than sex.

"Where do you stash the porno, Cookie?"

"THE DIRTY OLD MAN" GEEZER
(gezarius lecheris)

Identifiable by his sharpness of eye, the quick turn of his head, and his low whistle. Convinced that sex is basically a spectator sport. **Subscribes to:** *Playboy, Maxim* and *Penthouse.* **Proudest possession**: His extensive library of *Girls Gone Wild* videos. **Strongest belief**: That nothing is better than sex—if his memory is correct.

"*The air I breathe is filthy, my food is poisoned, my automobile is a gas-guzzling behemoth, my school taxes have doubled, the Internal Revenue Service plans to take the fillings out of my teeth, my wife is fifty-three and pregnant, my dog bit a lawyer's kid, my son steals, my mother-in-law is a Communist, my daughter ran off with a fink, and now you tell me that if I don't back up and let you have the right-of-way I'll be in trouble.*"

CHAPTER THREE

GEEZER PHILOSOPHY
(The Proper Geezer Outlook on Life Explained)

GEEZERS TEND TO have a personal philosophy, an outlook on life, and a mind-set that mark them apart from ordinary people. This philosophy is predicated on and underpinned by two basic core beliefs:

One: A geezer, while he knows that he does not know everything, also believes that he *does* know everything that is *worth* knowing.

Two: While a geezer does not expect everyone to always agree with him, he also believes that everyone has a responsibility to at least *try* to agree with him.

From these two core beliefs spring a subset of attitudes shared by most geezers the world over. Let's listen in on some typical geezer conversations and examine what they tell us about these admirable attitudes.

CONVERSATION #1
(Between a geezer and the passenger in his car.)

Passenger: It's perfectly obvious to me that we are hopelessly lost.

Geezer: Yeah, maybe. But we're making great time!

— • —

Consider the various attitudes evidenced in this brilliant reply.

Attitude #1: Disdain for the opinions of others.

If the geezer had simply agreed with his passenger that they were lost, he would have been acknowledging the passenger's superior appraisal of the situation. If the geezer *disagreed,* he would have been accepting his passenger's right to have an opinion. But in saying "Yeah, maybe," he is announcing clearly that he doesn't *care* what the passenger thinks. This is absolutely the proper attitude of a true geezer.

A. SCHWAB
Marriage Counsellor

"What's the word I want for that disposition of yours?"

Attitude #2: Inconsideration

The geezer's reply in this situation evidences a lack of consideration for his passenger. The passenger is probably trying to be helpful—but geezers don't like to be helped. His reply of "Yeah, maybe," is the perfect response. He has gently but firmly put the passenger in his place.

Attitude #3: Contrariness

In saying "But we're making great time!" the geezer is announcing that he doesn't really *care* if they're lost, particularly in light of the fact that the passenger has brought up the possibility. In all likelihood, if the passenger had said, "I think we're on the right road," the geezer would have disagreed and turned the car around.

Attitude #4: Obstinacy

It's worth noting that the geezer has not asked for or invited any consultation on how to reach his destination. The old saying, "Real men never ask directions," applies in spades to geezers. Geezers, to say the least, are set in their ways and in their opinions. Asking for advice is a clear sign of weakness. Being right is a way of life. And if a geezer is ever proven wrong, he will immediately try to find a way to sound as if he's in the right. For example: "But we're making great time."

"Grayson is a liberal in social matters, a conservative in economic matters, and a homicidal psychopath in political matters."

Attitude #5: Grumpiness

It can be assumed that there was at least a low-level snarl in the geezer's voice—a certain note of disdain and disagreeableness. "Yeah, maybe" can't really be said pleasantly. Here is the very essence of the geezer attitude toward life—and toward his fellow man. Grumpiness is a state of mind intrinsic to the geezer character. Without grumpiness a geezer is not truly fulfilled. You can be old without being grumpy—and you can be grumpy without being old. But to be old *and* grumpy is to be—a geezer!

Now let's consider another brief geezer conversation, this one between a geezer visiting California for the first time and a friend showing him one of the great West Coast views.

THE GEEZER CREDO

I cannot see
I cannot pee
I cannot chew
I cannot screw
My memory shrinks
My hearing stinks
No sense of smell
I look like hell
The Golden Years
Have come at last
The Golden Years
Can kiss my ass!
—Anon

CONVERSATION #2

Friend: There it is. The Pacific Ocean. Isn't that something?
Geezer (sourly): It's not as big as I thought it would be.

— • —

This wonderful reply evidences several important aspects of the geezer philosophy.

Attitude #6: Disappointment

What did the geezer expect? It doesn't matter. Most geezers are more or less hard-wired to be disappointed and are prepared to deal with it. The reply, "It isn't as big as I thought it would be," doesn't actually make any sense—

but it does communicate the idea that the geezer is hard to impress. After all, over the decades he has pretty much seen it all, heard it all, done it all. From this point on, life doesn't offer many surprises—much less happy ones.

And let's say that something happens that *doesn't* disappoint. There is even a geezer fall-back position for that: He can always be disappointed that he is not disappointed!

Of course, it's always possible that the geezer's vision has deteriorated with age and that the Pacific Ocean really doesn't look very big to him. But that's a whole other story.

"This is a hell of a way to run a railroad!
You call that a dry Martini?"

CONVERSATION #3
(Between a driver and his geezer passenger.)

Driver: Look at all those sheep out there on the hillside. They've been freshly shorn.

Geezer (thoughtfully): "Yeah. At least on this side."

— • —

Here we have evidence of still another aspect of the geezer philosophy.

Attitude #7: Skepticism

The geezer concedes nothing—disputes whenever possible—and always suspects the suppositions of others. He is often willing to challenge the seemingly unchallengeable. In this case, he wants to *see* the other side of those sheep before he is willing to accept the driver's statement. That's geezer skepticism at its best!

Attitude #8: Stubbornness

Geezers are known to dig in their heels on even the most minor points of contention. Even when faced with overwhelming logic, geezers can be remarkably...well... steadfast. The geezer knows that the odds are that all of those sheep *have* been shorn on all sides. But he has committed himself to the argument that they might not be—and you can rest assured he will not easily change his mind. Think of it as "tenacity of opinion"—and respect the geezer for his strength of will and toughness of mind.

Now let's consider one more geezer conversation.

CONVERSATION #4
(Between a geezer at his desk and his wife,
who is opening the mail.)

Wife: "No wonder you haven't paid the utility bills. Your desk is a terrible, disorganized mess."

Geezer: "Well, don't try straightening it up. I'll never be able to find anything!"

— • —

Here we see several other characteristics of the geezer philosophy that play an important role in full geezer living.

Attitude #9: The Joy of Messiness

There are neat geezers, to be sure. But most are schooled in the joy of messiness. It's not that they are *deliberately* untidy, it's just that constantly straightening, organizing, and picking up seem to cut unnecessarily into a geezer's remaining time. This attitude is not without merit. Recent studies show that people who said they keep a "very neat" desk spend an average of 36 percent more time looking for things than people who said they kept a "very messy desk." No less a personage than Albert Einstein once said, "If a cluttered desk is a sign of a cluttered mind, what then is an empty desk a sign of?"

Attitude #10: The Tendency Toward Stinginess

A great many geezers seem to have short arms and deep pockets. "Cheap" might be too strong a word, "tight" doesn't seem quite right either. Let's settle on "parsimonious," which means "possessing a predilection for extreme or unusual frugality."

After all, it only makes sense that a man who has worked hard all his life—and along the way developed a skeptical and unsympathetic attitude toward people and institutions

"It seems ridiculous to get rid of it now, with Christmas only a couple of months away."

in general—should be reluctant to squander his assets on those he considers undeserving.

So there it is—the geezer philosophy spelled out in all its glory. These are the stepping stones that, if followed, can lead to the full geezer lifestyle:

1. Disdain for the opinions of others
2. Contrariness
3. Obstinacy
4. Inconsideration
5. Grumpiness
6. Disappointment
7. Skepticism
8. Stubbornness
9. Messiness
10. Stinginess

Geezers who have not mastered them all should not be discouraged. Rome was not built in a day—and true geezerhood does not happen overnight. With perseverance, practice, will-power and determination, you too can be the geezer you've always dreamed of being. It will be worth the effort—and the rewards will be great. With luck, you will be able to frustrate and offend people for the rest of your life!

"Any minute now we're due for one of his outbursts of gloomy philosophy."

BEING TIGHTFISTED IS
THE HALLMARK OF A REAL GEEZER

Stinginess requires *technique*. And over the years, geezers have developed a wide variety of methods for avoiding unnecessary expenditure. Consider some of their secrets for keeping the expense of dining out with friends to a minimum:

- Promising to get the check "next time" (knowing full well there's not going to be a next time!).
- Carrying an expired credit card (and expressing shock, regret and disbelief when it is found to be unusable).
- Discovering that "nature calls" as the bill is on its way to the table. (Timing is of the essence!)
- Feigning illness immediately after the plates are removed. (This requires not inconsiderable acting skills and should be employed with discretion.)
- Claiming, at the precise moment of bill-arrival, that your vibrating cell phone has summoned you to an important call. (Useful only in restaurants that require you to exit the premises to talk.)
- Announcing dramatically that your wallet has been stolen. (This tactic not only saves participation in the bill-paying event, but also elicits sympathy and understanding.)
- Carrying large bills that cannot be changed by coat checkers and car parkers.

THE GEEZER CROSSWORD*

ACROSS

1. No geezer ever flew on a ____
6. Sea-parting geezer
10. Sometimes even a geezer feels his ____
11. Real geezers never dish the ____
12. Greedy sort
15. Every geezer loves a ____
17. Fruity drink
18. Unyielding, like a geezer
21. Itsy-bitsy
22. "You stink!"
23. A geezer pet peeve
27. Fraction of a lb.
28. Roman language
30. Paul of 1932's *Scarface*
31. Geezer walking aid
33. McDonald's geezer, Ray ____
34. Early car geezer

35. Alternative to .com, .edu or .net
36. Most geezers can't Hula-____
39. Emperor who rhymes with "geezer"
43. "Time ____ money"
45. Sticking up
48. ____ Day (May 8, 1945)
49. Popular geezer pastime
50. ____route (on the way)
51. Hairy Tibetan beast
52. Burn slightly
54. Outstanding grades
55. Rental agent
56. Geezer's monthly check: Abbr.
58. Iconic Indian geezer
61. A geezer's support system
64. Chicken ____ king
65. Med. school subj.
67. Runaway bride or groom
68. Himalayan land
69. A geezer cake has lots of these

DOWN

1. ____ and fro
2. Geezer popoff
3. "Fire ____ will"
4. "Mind your ____ and q's!"
5. Average geezer's sexual prospects
6. Playing marble
7. "... ____ quit!" (ultimatum ending)
8. Geezer book editor
9. Famous Irish playwright geezer
11. Geezer chewing aid
13. Popular theater name
14. An old guy with attitude

15. Certain NFL backfield member
16. Hesitation sound
18. Geezer pout
19. ____-date (modern)
20. The perfect geezer car
24. "____ what's more..."
25. Roman 11
26. Dickens geezer
29. An ____ and a leg (exorbitant cost)
30. Part of a yr.
32. Geezers were born a long time ____
34. American founder geezer
35. "____, no!" ("This can't be!")
37. Most geezers take lots of these
38. Bit of air rifle ammo
39. Undercover org.
40. Abbr. meaning "for example"
41. "We try harder" rental company
42. A geezer always prays that his driver's license will be ____
44. Viennese psychiatrist geezer's initials
45. American geezer president
46. Geezers save money when their purchases are ____
47. U.S. Senator geezer
52. Celebrating gift-giving geezer
53. Geezer boxer Foreman's product
57. A nimble geezer is often called ____
59. Geezer snooze
60. "2001" computer
62. "Friend or ____?"
63. Mini-albums, for short
66. A hot geezer can always turn on the ____

Warning: Anyone alert enough to do this puzzle may not be a geezer. Solution on next page.

THE GEEZER CROSSWORD SOLUTION

T	R	A	P	E	Z	E		M	O	S	E	S	
O	A	T	S		E		D	I	R	T		H	O	G
	N			F	R	E	E	B	I	E		A	D	E
S	T	U	B	B	O	R	N			V		W	E	E
U		P	U			T	A	X	E	S		O	Z
L	A	T	I	N		M	U	N	I		C	A	N	E
K	R	O	C		F	O	R	D		O	R	G		R
	M		K		R		E		H	O	O	P
	B		C	A	E	S	A	R		O		I	S
R	O	B	B	I	N	G		V	E		G	O	L	F
E	N		Y	A	K		S	I	N	G	E		L
A	S		R		L	E	A	S	E	R		S	S
G	A	N	D	H	I		N		W	I	F	E		P
A	L	A		A	N	A	T		E	L	O	P	E	R
N	E	P	A	L		C	A	N	D	L	E	S		Y

"I'd just like to know what in hell is happening, that's all. I'd like to know what in hell is happening! Do you know what in hell is happening?"

CHAPTER FOUR

GEEZER GAB
(How to Talk and Sound Like a Real Geezer)

M OST GEEZERS have a way of saying things that is all their own. A discerning person should be able to have a conversation with his eyes closed and still be able to tell whether or not he is talking to a true geezer.

Here, for instance, are a few snippets of conversation that should give you an idea of "geezerspeak."

The Situation: Two people meet on the street and the following greetings take place.

Person: How are you today?

Geezer: What? What? Speak up for God's sake!

Person: (slightly louder) I said— how are you today?

Geezer: Well, you don't have to *shout*!

The Situation: Two people are discussing a recent political development.

Person: Have you made up your mind about it yet?

Geezer: Absolutely not!

Person: You haven't?

Geezer: No. But when I do, I'm going to be good and damned mad about it!

The Situation: A salesman is trying to sell an elderly farmer a book on the latest farming techniques.

Salesman: Aren't you interested in buying it?

Geezer: Of course not!

Salesman: Why not?

Geezer: 'Cause I ain't farmin' now as good as I know how!

Now let's consider the various components of these three conversations.

The Confrontation

At the first opportunity, the geezer has challenged the other speaker—sharply—and put him on notice that he, the geezer, is going to dominate and control the conversation.

"Speak up, for God's sake!"

"Absolutely not!"

"Of course not!"

The aggressive statement by the geezer then dictates a predictably timid and defensive reaction from the other person.

"I said—how are you today?"

"You haven't?"

"Why not?"

The geezer is now in complete control of the conversation and ready to finish off his fellow conversationalist with a declarative statement for which there is absolutely no response. This is called:

The Zap

"Well, you don't have to *shout!*"

"When I do, I'm going to be good and damned mad about it!"

"Cause I ain't farmin' now as good as I know how!"

There is now clearly nothing left to be said. The other speaker will probably, at this point, slink away quietly.

Once a geezer has established primacy in a conversation, he can then move forward and employ other techniques of geezerspeak.

The Rant

Geezers can be quick to anger and insightful in detecting slights and insults from others. They are also usually quick to respond. Geezers-in-training note: This is when the rant can be useful. Rants require an increase in vocal volume, a speeding up of word delivery and, if at all possible, a reddening of the face. If a cane is at the ready, it can be waved about for added emphasis.

Rants need not be confined to a certain subject, as witnessed by the very excellent geezer rant from the cartoon that opens Chapter Three.

> "The air I breathe is filthy, my food is poisoned, my automobile is a gas-guzzling behemoth, my school taxes have doubled , the Internal Revenue Service plans to take the fillings out of my teeth, my wife is fifty-three and pregnant, my dog bit a lawyer's kid, my son steals, my mother-in-law is a Communist, my daughter ran off with a fink, and now *you* tell me that if I don't back up and let you have the right-of-way I'll be in trouble."

This particular rant could well be considered a model for any geezer to follow. It has all the necessary ingredients: a rush of words, an apparently loud delivery, and a genuine tone of outrage. Only the waving cane is missing, and this should be excused because the geezer involved was confined to his automobile. This is, clearly, a model worth emulating.

The Whine

Most geezers are inclined to a certain degree of self-pity. This is certainly understandable. After all, most geezers have endured a mountain of abuse over the years. They've endured the indignities of life. Geezer whines should be delivered in a somewhat softer voice than rants. They should be shorter in length and they should be confined to a single subject. Consider these five very excellent whines:

"Why do these things always happen to me?"
"Can't you see I'm *busy*?"
"Is that the best you can do?"
"How long has *this* been going on?"
"Don't you ever *listen*?"

Geezer whines do not need to be real complaints. In fact, if they are contrived, they can be all the more effective—as witnessed by this geezer's absolutely brilliant whine:

"Do you think I like being a hypochondriac?"

This particular whine has everything. It is short and to the point. It poses an unanswerable question. Made from the sickbed, it indicates personal suffering. And, finally, it is accusatory—putting the blame clearly on the recipient of the whine.

With practice, any geezer should be able to achieve this level of whining. One note of caution: Except in unusual circumstances, the average geezer should be content with two or three whines per day. Too much whining can be unattractive. Ten or more whines in a single day should be considered excessive.

The Sarcasm

Most geezers know the value of the sarcastic remark. It not only puts the rival conversationalist in his place, but it demonstrates the superior mental capabilities of the geezer. Let's take a look at a few classic geezer sarcasms.

Man: Sometimes I think I'm my own worst enemy.

Geezer: Not while I'm alive, you aren't.

— • —

Young Man: How dare you accuse me. Have you ever heard my honesty questioned?

Geezer: I've never even heard it mentioned.

— • —

Patient: Doctor, another physician I have consulted disagrees with your diagnosis, and I'm going to go with his recommendation.

Geezer Doctor: Fine. But I'm sure the autopsy will prove I'm right.

— • —

| Wife: | It's your son's birthday next week. What are you going to do for him? |
| Geezer: | I'm going to pretend to be dangerously ill. |

— • —

| Man: | I understand Harry is getting hard of hearing. |
| Geezer: | Yeah. Lack of practice. |

— • —

| Man: | I passed your house yesterday while I was out walking. |
| Geezer: | I appreciate that. |

— • —

These examples should give guidance to the geezer in constructing his own sarcasms. Remember that the essence of the successful sarcasm is brevity combined with wit. As valuable as sarcasm is in the geezer's vocal weaponry, it is not always adequate to the task. There are some situations that require a more direct approach and stronger words. This is when he should turn to. . .

The Stopper

Most geezers are masters of expressing strong disapproval. And for good reason. Geezers have lots to upset them and to provoke anger: Unappreciative wives, annoying neighbors, pushy strangers, noisy children, and, worst of all, people who disagree with them.

Because of this, geezers often need a technique stronger than sarcasm to deal with certain situations involving these kinds of people. They need "stoppers"!

GEEZERS CAN REMEMBER WHEN...

"Gay" meant happy, charming and light-hearted.

"Crack" meant the sound of something breaking.

"CD's" meant Certificates of Deposit.

"Draft dodger" meant someone getting away from the wind.

"Time sharing" meant spending quality time with your buddies.

"Discs" meant parts of the spinal column.

"Spam" meant a can of mediocre meat.

"Grass" meant that green stuff that you mowed.

"Coke" meant a bottle of soda.

"Pot" meant a container you cooked stuff in.

"Ho" meant a gardening implement.

"Chips" meant small chunks of wood.

"Stoppers" need not be subtle or clever. They need only to be clear and emphatic. Here are some examples that have proven useful and effective over the years:

"Get the hell out of here!"

"Shut up!"

"You can go straight to hell!"

"Don't give me any of that shit!"

"Don't be so stupid!"

"In a pig's eye!"

"Bullshit!"

Stopper phrases generally conclude any attempt at further discussion and permit the geezer to finish the conversation with a sense of triumph and finality.

Not all people engaged in conversation with geezers are offensive or disagreeable. Many of them will be simply, well, boring. This leads logically to a geezer ploy known as...

The Great "Whatever"

It is important for a geezer to know how to shut down (and up!) an overly active conversationalist (particularly on the part of a non-geezer). After all, a geezer's time may be limited and he doesn't want to spend too much of it listening to a bore. There are a number of ways to accomplish this.

1. Adopt a facial expression indicating total disinterest.
2. Simply stare off in another direction.
3. Begin looking for something in your wallet.
4. Conspicuously turn off your hearing aid.
5. Feign going to sleep.
6. Abruptly leave the room.

Unfortunately, any of these tactics might be considered rude. A far better method is to simply wait until the bore pauses to take a breath and then say, quietly but firmly: "Whatever."

This gently informs the speaker that his time is up and that you had no interest in the subject in the first place. There is no way for him to continue speaking right after hearing this magical word. And while he ponders the significance of "whatever," the geezer has ample time to begin his own boring monologue.

There are some things said by geezers that mean something else altogether. It is important for ordinary people to know what these are to avoid misunderstandings. Following are just a few . . .

A GEEZER SAYS	A GEEZER MEANS
When I was your age...	Please prepare yourself for a long, boring story.
I know *exactly* where we are!	We're lost!
That's a crock!	If you're right, I don't want to know it.
In a pig's eye!	If I'm wrong, I don't want to hear about it.
I was just resting my eyes.	That was a great nap!
I can't hear myself think!	I hate your music—if that's what you call it!
I'm not a morning person.	I'll do it later, much later!
Do you think I'm *made* of money?	If you want it you can buy it yourself!
Would you say that again?	Where were you when brains were passed out?
Do you have any *more* good ideas?	Drop dead!
They don't make 'em like that anymore.	It's a relic, but I'm not getting rid of it.

HOW A GEEZER SHOULD TELL A STORY

Most geezers are notorious, even feared, storytellers. Some claim that spending an evening with a loquacious geezer is a fate rivaling death. As a geezer, you have a responsibility to sustain and uphold this valued tradition:

1. **Make certain that all or almost all of the audience members have heard the story before.** If they are friends or relatives, this will probably not be a problem. If they have heard it more than once, so much the better.

2. **Be sure that the telling of the story is, for want of a better term, interminable.** Use a factor of ten as a "rule of thumb." If, for example, the story could be told in one minute, it should be stretched out to ten minutes. A two minute story should take at least twenty, and so forth. This will be an invaluable aid in achieving geezer greatness in the telling of tales. This is not difficult to master with a little practice. Leave out no unnecessary detail—time of day, color of the sky, whatever superfluous minutia that can be worked into the story.

3. **Develop the habit of ignoring any signs of inattention on the part of the audience:** Glazed eyes, coughing, shifting of the feet, even mild snoring. These signs of weakness on the part of the listeners should, in fact, spur you on to even greater loquaciousness.

4. **Always remember, at the end of the story, to pause dramatically, and then to say**—"That's it in a nutshell!"

CONCLUSION

Most geezers can talk "geezerspeak" like experts, naturally and without difficulty or hesitation. Fledgling or apprentice geezers may need some study and practice—but an occasional review of the foregoing material can prove helpful until full fluency is achieved. Like most things in life—practice makes perfect!

"Harry insisted on doing everything himself."

GEEZER GAFFES
(Some Historic Mistakes by Memorable Geezers)

IT IS NOT THAT geezers are more accident prone than younger people, who are perhaps more agile of mind and body. It's just that most geezers have had more experience at making mistakes. Through trial and error, success and failure, they've learned over the years how to err with panache, with a certain élan, that younger people have not yet mastered.

Now we're not talking minor everyday mistakes—like forgetting an appointment or calling your wife by the wrong name. No, we're talking about the grander, more creative, more memorable mistakes—the kind that make the birds take flight and the angels cringe.

On the following pages are some outstanding examples of geezer gaffes that have occurred over the years. They make for joyous, if disturbing, reading.

President Martin Van Buren, long after he had retired from office, wrote an extensive and detailed biography of his political career and his personal life. After it was published, he looked through it—only to discover that he had made a serious omission: He completely forgot to mention that he was married and had four children.

— • —

A geezer in Germany was electrocuted while trying to kill moles in his garden with a high voltage cable. The elderly gentleman was found dead on the ground at his country home in Zingst. Lying nearby was a live 380-volt power cable and a number of metal spikes had been driven into the ground. A police spokesman said the man had resorted to "an unorthodox method to get rid of moles."

"The moles survived," he added.

— • —

In his later years, the great mid-nineteenth century actor Junius Booth was still a dependable performer, but age had dimmed his organizational skills. One night, before a performance, he was wandering aimlessly backstage when he finally located a stagehand. "Where do I make my entrance?" he asked. The stagehand piloted him to the place in the wings. Then, just before he stepped on stage, he turned to his benefactor and said, "And what's the play tonight?"

— • —

Late in the nineteenth century, the elderly Emperor of Abyssinia, eager to let his subjects know that he was serious about the subject of crime in the country, ordered three new electric chairs. After they arrived, his advisors cautiously reminded him that Abyssinia had no electricity.

— • —

An elderly and eccentric preacher in the West African nation of Gabon, after a week of prayer and meditation, announced to his parishioners that God had granted him the power to walk on water, just as Jesus had. Accordingly, an assembly of friends and well-wishers gathered on the shore the next day to witness the first exercise of this extraordinary new gift. As one witness later reported, "He walked right into the water and kept going until he disappeared. We haven't seen him since."

— • —

German police stopped an elderly man they clocked doing 40 mph in his souped-up electric wheelchair. Guenther Eichman, 74, told them he was a retired engineer and had modified the wheelchair to make it zoom. Police failed to see the humor in it, confiscated the vehicle and fined Eichman $600. Said Eichman in protest, "I thought the speed limit here was 50!"

— • —

An elderly preacher in rural England, unfamiliar with the new technologies afforded today's orators, left a service for a trip to the men's room, not realizing that he was still wearing his cordless microphone. Suddenly, the church was filled with splashing sounds, followed by an audible sigh of relief, followed by loud sounds of flushing. Said one parishioner following the service, "It was most embarrassing. I don't know if anyone has yet had the courage to tell him."

— • —

The aging and eccentric multi-millionaire, William Randolph Hearst, sent one of his assistants to Europe to try to find a classical statue that he wanted to add to his collection. After scouring the continent for several months, he finally returned empty-handed. An impatient Hearst demanded to know why the assistant had not located the item he lusted after. The assistant explained that while he had not returned with it, he had determined its location and ownership: Hearst himself had purchased it years earlier and it was stored in his warehouse in Los Angeles.

— • —

On the occasion of his eightieth birthday, Somerset Maugham, the celebrated writer and raconteur, was called on at the end of a lavish and liquid dinner to make a speech. "There are many rewards," he began, "in growing old." Then he paused, looked reflectively out at the audience, and gazed skyward, stretching the pause into a long, awkward silence. At last, he cleared his throat and continued, "But, at the moment," he said, "I can't remember any of them."

— • —

The Scottish writer, John Campbell, well into his dotage, bought a book that attracted his attention. He took it home and read a goodly portion of it, agreeing with everything it said. When he finally took the time to see who the author was, he discovered the reason he found the book so agreeable. He had written it himself.

— • —

A judge in Finland ruled that a geezer had seriously erred in agreeing to pay $32,000 to touch a woman's breasts. The case involved a woman in her 20s who charged a 74-year-old man 25,500 euros ($32,000) for permitting him to touch both of her breasts. Judge Hasse Hakki ruled that she had bilked the old gentleman and sentenced her to a year in jail. "Based on general life experience alone," said the judge, "it is indisputably clear that the charge was greatly disproportionate to the service rendered."

— • —

A 75-year-old geezer in Tennessee sued local authorities for $1.5 million after they raided his house and removed 114 dead, frozen cats. He claimed "emotional pain and suffering" because their actions frustrated his desire to get into the Guinness Book of Records.

— • —

When poet W. H. Auden was about to delivery a lecture at the New School for Social Research, he cautioned the crowd as follows, "If there is anyone here who has trouble hearing me, don't bother raising your hand as I am also terribly near-sighted."

— • —

When Adolph Zukor, the great film mogul, granted an interview on his 103rd birthday, the first question the interviewer asked him was, "Why do you think you have lived so long?" Replied Zukor, "I quit smoking two years ago."

TEN SONGS FOR AND ABOUT GEEZERS

September Song
I'm Old Fashioned
When You Grow Too Old to Dream
I'm So Glad I'm Not Young Anymore
Golden Slumbers
It's So Hard to Remember
Old Black Joe
Things Ain't What They Used to Be
Don't Get Around Much Anymore
I Can't Remember Where or When

*"By God, for a minute there
it suddenly all made sense!"*

CHAPTER SIX

GEEZER WISDOM
(Wise Sayings By the Wisest Geezers)

G EEZERS DOWN through the decades have been
generous in sharing their accumulated
wisdom with ordinary people. Following are
some selected examples of their keenness of
mind, their shrewdness of perception, and their
profundity of thought.

"I think I've acquired some wisdom
over the years, but there doesn't seem
to be much demand for it."

"As the days dwindle down to a precious few, I've decided not to take any shit."   —George Burns

"Health nuts are going to feel stupid someday, lying in hospitals dying of nothing."   —Redd Foxx

"After seventy, it's just patch, patch, patch."
                                        —Jimmy Stewart

"Old age is the most unexpected thing that ever happened to me."   —Leon Trotsky

"At a formal dinner party, the person nearest death should always be seated closest to the bathroom."
                                        —George Carlin

"Don't worry about avoiding temptation. As you get older, it will avoid you."   —Anon

"Old age is a very high price to pay for maturity."
                                        —Tom Stoppard

"An eccentric is a man who is too rich to be called a crackpot."
                                        —C.B. Ascot

"No matter how old you are, you're younger than you'll ever be again."   —Anon.

"The young have aspirations that never come to pass; the old have reminiscences of what never happened."
                                        —La Rochefoucould

"The trouble is that the young don't know what to do—and the old can't do what they know."—Groucho Max

"No pleasure is worth giving up for the sake of two more years in a geriatric home.'"   —Kingsley Amis

"I knew I was going bald because it took me longer and longer to wash my face."   —Benny Hill

"A senior citizen is a guy who can remember when a senior citizen was called an 'old timer.'" —William Ashley

"Growing old is mandatory. Growing up is optional."
                    —Chili Davis

"When I told my doctor I couldn't afford an operation, he offered to touch up my X-rays."   —Henry Youngman

"I get my exercise acting as pallbearer to my friends who exercise."   —Chauncey Depew

"Avoid running at all times."   —Satchel Paige

"I don't want to achieve immortality through my work. I want to achieve it by not dying."   —Woody Allen

"Old age is when you feel like the morning after the night before and you haven't been anywhere."
                    —Dean Martin

"Growing old is like being increasingly penalized for a crime you didn't commit."   —Anthony Powell

GEEZER ALERT!

The Greek goddess Era was given one wish— and she selected eternal life. And so she did live forever. She got old, then older, then even older, until she became ancient, shriveled, weak, demented and wracked with pain. So if you are ever granted just one wish by a fairy or a genie, remember not to ask for eternal life. Ask for eternal *youth*!

SEVEN GREAT GEEZER NEW YEAR'S RESOLUTIONS

1. Diet until you weigh what it says on your driver's license (if you still have one!).

2. Get some new teeth (that whistling is annoying!).

3. Clip those nose hairs. (some people think you have a moustache!).

4. Try a new way to hide your bald spot (that comb-over looks terrible!).

5. Call up an old friend (if you still have one!).

6. Try Viagra (but forget that four hour thing—settle for four minutes!).

7. Do something nice for an enemy (it will drive him crazy!).

"They say the first things to go are your legs and your eyesight. It isn't. The first thing to go is parallel parking."
—Kurt Vonnegut

"You know you're getting old when your wife believes your excuses for getting home late."   —Basil Ransome-Davies

"Senescence starts and old age begins when your descendents outnumber your friends."   —Ogden Nash

"By the time you're old enough to know what's going on, you're not going anywhere."   —Ed Howe

"A touch of deafness lightens one's heaviest chores—listening to bores."   —Ogden Nash

"The last thing a man wants to do is—the last thing he does."
—Anon.

"I'm ordinarily patient, provided I get my way in the end."
—John Simone

"There is one thing women can never take away from men. We die sooner." —P.J. O'Rourke

"One of the blessings of old age is that people tend to overlook your foibles—which can ease the task of being rude and unpleasant." —Chester A. Longworth

"You know the years are hurrying by when it takes you longer to rest up than it did to get tired." —Philip Aschew

"A real geezer only chases girls if it's downhill." —Charles Witherbottom

"Whenever you think you would like to go back to your youth—think of algebra!" —T. Harnsworthy

"I can't figure out how I got over the hill without ever getting to the top." —James T. Roth

"Old age is like everything else. To make a success of it, you've got to start young." —Fred Astaire

A GEEZER'S REGRET

I've come to accept my graying hair
And each new wrinkle I find.
I'm accustomed to the paunch in front
And the extra pounds behind.

I've learned to live with my arthritis
To dentures I'm resigned.
I've adjusted well to my bifocals
But God! How I miss my mind!

"You've got mail."

CHAPTER SEVEN

GREAT MOMENTS IN GEEZER HISTORY
(The Events that Shaped the World of Grumpiness)

THERE CAN BE NO doubt but that geezers have made significant contributions to mankind over the centuries. It is also true that certain events have impacted the lives of geezers in ways that have had lasting and dramatic effect. Following is a timeline denoting the most important of these contributions and events. Each marks an important date in geezer history—and together they constitute a roll call of the greatest moments in the geezer legend.

50,000 B.C.

Neanderthal geezer invents
the wheel, but idiotically
fails to apply for a patent.

12,000 B.C.

Biblical geezer Moses
presents The Ten
Commandments, solidifying
his reputation as the grump
of the millennium.

11 cent. A.D.

Scottish monks invent
distilled whiskey.

1492

Columbus discovers America,
and, more importantly, also
discovers tobacco.

1541

Michelangelo, renaissance geezer, paints the Sistine Chapel while lying on his back.

1657

Pierre Fauchard, a French dentist, invents false teeth.

1758

Benjamin Franklin, famous Philadelphia geezer and tinkerer with nature, invents bifocals.

1819

Washington Irving writes *Rip Van Winkle,* giving credence to the efficacies of the afternoon nap.

1873

Thomas Crapper, English crackpot geezer, invents the flush toilet.

1910

Simon deBaudelair, French writer, announces that at the age of 88 he makes love to his 90-year-old wife an average of four times a week.

1933

The Volstead Act establishing prohibition in the United States is repealed.

1935

Congress passes the Social Security Act.

1938

Walt Disney creates "Grumpy" and the other dwarfs, proving once and for all that geezers can be lovable.

1956

Zenith introduces the television remote control.

1957

The Laz-E-Boy Chair goes into national distribution.

1980

Ronald Reagan becomes the first geezer president, later the oldest living ex-president geezer.

1997

The Federal Drug Administration approves Viagra, making it possible for geezers everywhere to be upstanding citizens.

2004

Philip Rabinowitz, of Cape Town South Africa, sets a new record for the 100-meter sprint by 100-year-olds at 30.86 seconds.

*"I hate to mention it, but you've got
his coat buttoned the wrong way."*

CHAPTER EIGHT

GEEZER ROLE MODELS
(A Pantheon of Geezerhood at Its Greatest)

G EEZERS, LIKE everyone else, need role models—people they can admire and study in order to ascertain the ingredients of success.

That's why it is useful and instructive to recall the truly great geezers of the past. These are men who, through their antiquity, their eccentricities and their overall grumpiness have made their mark in world history. The pantheon of the "greats" is populated with some of the most remarkable figures ever to walk the earth.

Geezer greatness can be found among biblical figures, political leaders, titans of industry, entertainment stars, and sports heroes—as well as in literature and mythology.

On the following pages you will find our nominations for:

THE GEEZER HALL OF FAME

ABRAHAM (no last name) (before recorded time)

A truly great religious geezer.

Progenitor of the Hebrews and founder of both a faith and a people. Bears the title of Father of the Faithful and Friend of God. Perhaps the most significant of all biblical figures, he is reputed to have lived for hundreds of years, qualifying him for geezerhood on that count alone. Perhaps the progenitor of all geezers.

Greatest Eccentricity
Continually gazing skyward.

Grumpiest Act
Inventing and promulgating the practice of circumcision.

KING ARTHUR (dates unknown)
Prototype royal geezer.

The illegitimate son of Uther Pendragon, King of England, Arthur succeeded to the throne after performing the magical act of drawing a sword from a stone. Reigning in a place called Camelot, he proved to be a fine king and a mighty warrior. He was surrounded by noble knights (Lancelot and Tristan), but also by conniving evil-doers (Mordred and Morgan le Fay). A love affair between Lancelot and Arthur's wife, Guinevere, dimmed his enthusiasm for things chivalrous. Finally wounded in battle, he was borne away to the isle of Avalon where he died.

Greatest Eccentricity
Always insisted that his friends sit at a round table.

Grumpiest Act
Invented the chastity belt.

NOSTRADAMUS (1503–66)
A predicting geezer.

A.K.A. Michel de Nostradame, a French astrologer and physician, he is primarily famous for his vague and elliptical predictions regarding the fate and future of the world. Originally made his fame affecting remarkable cures during outbreaks of a plague in southern France. His celebrity apparently went to his head, and he began writing prophecies under the title "Centuries." He got lucky with his early predictions, which earned him enough of a following that he became a favorite of the royal court. His later prophecies were sufficiently vague and all-encompassing that modern scholars can read into them what they will.

Greatest Eccentricity
Making all his predictions in rhymed iambic pentameter.

Grumpiest Act
Predicting the end of the world.

JULIUS II (1443–1513)

The ultimate papal geezer.

A pope of the Roman Catholic Church, he was born Guiliano dello Rovere in Savona. He was the nephew of a pope (Sixtus IV), and was eventually made a Cardinal by his uncle. He thereupon, bewilderingly, made it his mission to stamp out nepotism in the Church. Also took on the mission of restoring the Papal States, and in that cause showed himself to be a commendable warrior. He went to war with Venice and won a number of military victories. Lived to be 70, an astonishing accomplishment in those turbulent times.

Greatest Eccentricity

Kept demanding bigger and bigger churches. Finally had to be content laying the cornerstone to St. Peters.

Grumpiest Act

Made Michelangelo lie on his back for four years painting a ceiling.

BENJAMIN FRANKLIN (1706–1790)

A great American founder geezer.

Diplomat, author, scientist, parliamentarian and coiner of wise sayings. Once flew a kite into a storm and thereby invented the lightning rod. Also invented the Franklin stove and bifocal glasses. Primarily known as a founding father, he was a delegate to the Continental Congress and a member of the committee that wrote the Declaration of Independence. As the American Ambassador to France, he negotiated the Treaty of Paris which established recognition of the United States as a nation. Spent his later years writing his autobiography so everyone would know how great he was.

Greatest Eccentricity

Walking around with a gnarled cane that looked like a dead tree.

Grumpiest Act

Wrote *Poor Richard's Almanac,* recommending hard work, discipline and restraint as the route to success.

EBENEZER SCROOGE (19th century)
The classic English literary geezer.

Scrooge was the invention of English writer Charles Dickens, who introduced his masterful "A Christmas Carol" in 1843. A prototype geezer, Scrooge was obsessed with the making and keeping of money. He worked his employees, especially Bob Cratchit, into a state of exhaustion, while paying them pauper's wages. Noted for his disdain for the poor and his frequent outrages. Finally softened up when visited by some Christmas ghosts.

Greatest Eccentricity
Counting his money over and over again.

Grumpiest Act
Insisting that Cratchit work on Christmas Day.

GEORGE BERNARD SHAW (1856–1950)
A monumental playwright geezer.

Aged, irascible and sarcastic, Shaw was one of England's and Ireland's greatest playwrights and literary figures. His plays were filled with impudence and wit, but struck unpopular social themes. His most memorable works were "Arms and the Man," "Mrs. Warren's Profession," "Man and Superman," "Saint Joan," "Androcles and the Lion," and of course, "Pygmalion" (later turned into the musical "My Fair Lady"). Shaw received the Nobel Prize in Literature in 1925. Lived well into his nineties and looked it. Cranky to the core.

Greatest Eccentricity
Unprovoked, one-way letter writing to beautiful women (Ellen Terry, Mrs. Patrick Campbell, etc.).

Grumpiest Act
Forced Eliza Doolittle, against her wishes, to learn a foreign language.

"Now can you hear me—you boys in the back?"

MAHATMA GANDHI (1869–1948)

Iconic pacifist geezer.

A geezer who really looked the part. Mohandas K. Gandhi is regarded as the father of modern India. A man of singular determination and habits, he exacted concessions from the English running the country because of the widespread devotion of his followers. He also forced some of India's princely states to adopt democratic reforms, and worked for the establishment of industries that would support the common workers of India. He advocated the elimination of "untouchability" for the lowest members of the caste system. He eventually achieved independence for his country—only to be assassinated by his enemies. Immortalized in film by actor Ben Kingsley.

Greatest Eccentricity

Frequently went weeks without eating.

Grumpiest Act

Suggested other people go weeks without eating.

JOHN D. ROCKEFELLER (1839–1937)
Number One petroleum geezer.

As an American industrialist and philanthropist, Rockefeller created the great Standard Oil Trust through mergers and buyouts of other petroleum interests. In outstanding geezer fashion, he ruthlessly crushed less able opponents and plundered their reserves and resources. Prominent also in the affairs of banks and railroads, he retired in 1911 as one of the wealthiest people in the world. Lived to be almost 100, a great geezer accomplishment in itself.

Greatest Eccentricity
Always dressed in black from hat to shoes.

Grumpiest Act
Always tipped people for services with a bright, shiny dime.

CASEY STENGEL (1891–1975)

Greatest of all sports geezers.

A grumpy, garrulous, cranky and spectacularly successful American baseball player and manager. As a player with Brooklyn, Pittsburgh, Philadelphia, New York, Boston, he compiled a respectable .284 batting average. Achieved his greatest fame as manager for the New York Yankees. Under his leadership, the team won ten league championships and seven world series—and he coached such luminaries as Roger Maris, Mickey Mantle, Joe DiMaggio and Whitey Ford. After he retired from baseball, he became a banker as well as a popular commercial figure.

Greatest Eccentricity

Insisted on mangling the English language.

Grumpiest Act

Saying that the 1961 World Series Champion Yankees were "the least bad team I ever coached."

FIDEL CASTRO (1927–)

A revolutionary geezer.

Imprisoned in Cuba early in life for an attack on the establishment, he was later released and went to Mexico where he organized the "26th of July" movement. He then led a group of invaders and eventually overthrew the existing government. He proceeded to institute collective agriculture, to expropriate all native and foreign industry, and to promote close ties with the U.S.S.R. and China. Finally, in 1961, he flatly stated he was a Marxist-Leninist. For more than fifty years, he ruled Cuba with an iron fist, railed against "Yankee Imperialism" and refused to change out of his old army uniform.

Greatest Eccentricity

Loved to make long-winded, boring speeches.

Grumpiest Act

Made people listen to his long-winded, boring speeches.

HENRY FORD (1863–1947)
The ultimate industrial geezer.

An American industrialist and pioneer automobile manufacturer, he was born in Dearborn, Michigan. He founded the Ford Motor Company in 1903, and eventually became the world's largest producer of autos. His most famous car was the Model T, which was purchased by more than fifteen million customers. He pioneered the modern assembly line and instituted a five-dollar-a-day wage for his workers, an unheard of wage at the time. He also introduced the eight hour work day. In later life, Ford was noted for his many quirks and idiosyncrasies.

Greatest Eccentricity
Collecting Jew's harps.

Grumpiest Act
Insisting all cars should be black.

DON QUIXOTE (16th century)
A beloved Spanish literary geezer.

Quixote roamed through sixteenth century Spain on a notable and memorable series of adventures and quests. An eccentric, he envisioned himself as a knight in shining armor, even though he traveled about in tacky garb while straddling an old ramshackle horse. Usually carried a lance for effect, and traveled with a comical sidekick named Sancho Panza. Originally created by Spanish writer and dramatist Cervantes, he was later immortalized in the Broadway musical "Man of La Mancha." No known descendants.

Greatest Eccentricity
Kept dreaming the impossible dream, over and over again.

Grumpiest Act
Constantly attacking windmills.

"I hope this isn't meant to be a criticism of our current life style."

MOSES (no last name) (13th century B.C.)
The perfect biblical geezer.

A Hebrew lawgiver and prophet. As a young man, he received his calling from a burning bush. Later in life, he led Israel out of Egypt and across the desert. In his old age, God gave him a peek at the Promised Land from the top of Mt. Pisgah. He lived to a ripe old age, revered by his people and today is admired as one of the greatest religious figures of all time. Died penniless and was buried in Moab. Played in films by Charlton Heston.

Greatest Eccentricity
Making the Jews march through the desert for forty years—to the only place in the Middle East that doesn't have oil.

Grumpiest Act
Gave mankind the ten commandments.

SANTA CLAUS (immortal)
Prototype mythical geezer.

A.K.A. Saint Nicholas. He first showed up in the fourth century as the Bishop of Myra in Asia Minor, and his career really took off from there! Somewhere along the line, he morphed into Santa, grew a white beard and started wearing red clothes and a red peaked hat. Reputedly now resides in the North Pole with his eternal bride, Mrs. Claus. Raises reindeer and surrounds himself with elves, whom he forces to make toys all year. Ventures out only once a year and makes a grand tour of the world, dispensing gifts and happiness. Thought of highly by small children.

Greatest Eccentricity
Insists on entering houses through the chimney.

Grumpiest Act
Refusing to give any presents to anyone who hasn't been "good."

GEORGE BURNS (1895–1996)

Iconic comedian geezer.

A radio, television and movie performer for more than seventy years, Burns was the grand old geezer of American entertainment. He originally starred in vaudeville with his partner, and later his spouse, Gracie Allen, then performed in radio on "The George Burns and Gracie Allen Show" for twenty-eight years. Their television show ran successfully for a decade. After his wife's death, Burns turned to stage performances and films. Starred in more than thirty films over a fifty year period, winning an Academy Award as Best Supporting Actor.

Greatest Eccentricity

Occasionally pretended to be God (in films, of course).

Grumpiest Act

At age 95, refused to sign a five-year contract with Caesar's Palace, saying he couldn't be sure Caesar's Palace would be there in five years!

"Stop saying I'll live to be ninety. I am ninety."

CHAPTER NINE

GEEZER LONGEVITY

(How to Be a Geezer for a Long Time)

ONCE A GEEZER, always a geezer. True. But, if a geezer can't go back—that still leaves the question of how long a geezer can go on! Forever, perhaps? Well, it's not likely... but still...

WHO SAYS YOU'VE GOT TO DIE?

Good question. Well, there are the historians, of course. They are always quick to cite the fact that people have been dying for centuries. And wouldn't they be embarrassed if you *didn't*!

Then there's your *doctor*. He'll be quick to tell you that you're not going to live forever. But if you stop to think about it, he has a vested interest in your dying. If you thought you weren't going to die, what would you need with *him*?

And, of course, there are your *heirs*. They would be *distraught* if they thought you weren't going to go.

So perhaps it's time to take a serious scientific look at the likelihood that you are—or are not—going to live forever.

Consider this: It has been estimated that fifty billion people have been born on this planet. That's a lot of folks. And then consider this: Some six billion of these people are

*"Donald is such a fatalist—he's convinced
he's going to grow old and die."*

still alive! Six out of fifty. That means that 12 percent of all human beings ever born are still walking around.

It is, therefore, a simple mathematical calculation to determine that your odds on dying are 8 to 1. Or, looking at it from the "glass half full" point of view—1 out of 8 that you're *not* going to die! Those may not be great odds—but at least they give you a shot at immortality!

Here is yet another way to look at your prospects: *The life expectancy formula.* Actuaries all agree that at age 80 your life expectancy is 8 years. Not so good. But when 88, your life expectancy is 4 years. And when you're 92, your life expectancy is 2 years. And so on. Even when you're 100, you're life expectancy is 1 year. In other words, it is a mathematical certainty that, no matter how old you are, you will *always* have a statistical life expectancy. If you make it to 110, it may be only one day. But that's okay. Take it!

Now it may be that even after those very powerful arguments, you still prefer to believe in the "death theory." That's understandable. After all, acceptance of the idea of never dying requires a contemplation of "infinity," which can lead to serious headache and even, in some cases, to a severe rash.

Besides, most people actually *want* to die. A recent poll by USA Today/ABC News determined that the average person would like to live to age 87. Only 25 percent want to live to be 100 or older. And only 7 percent expressed a desire to live forever.

So if you're one of those who is determined to die, at least you want to live as long as you can—and to have some idea of what is going to do you in.

On the following page you will find a chart showing what the odds are for meeting your maker in certain circumstances.

THE EXIT ODDS:

Here are the ways to say "adios"—and the odds that
each will happen to you. It's worth a look!

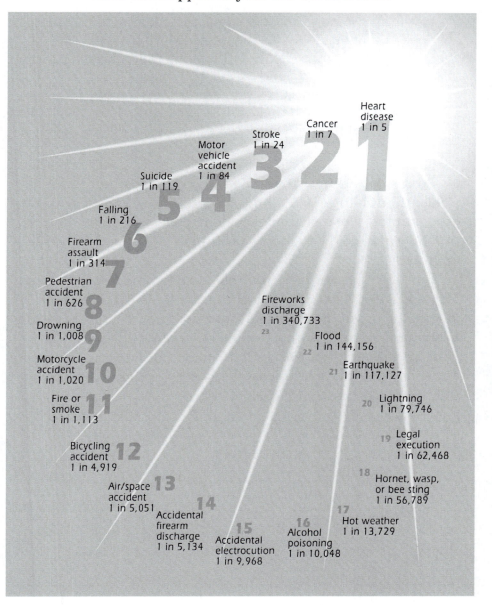

THE TERMINAL GEEZER

A geezer got a phone call from his doctor. The doctor said, "I've got some bad news— and some even worse news." "What's the bad news?" asked the geezer? "Your tests show you have just 24 hours to live," said the doctor. "Good lord," said the geezer. "What could be even worse news than that?" Replied the doctor, "I've been trying to get hold of you since yesterday!"

So now you know the odds. Yes, riding a motorcycle is riskier than riding a bike—and the odds on legal electrocution are infinitely greater than accidental electrocution. You're probably not going to worry too much about any of those anyway.

But take a closer look at stroke, cancer and heart attack. The odds there look far more troubling. And the question is—what can you do to help avoid those possibilities beyond avoiding motorcycles and electric chairs? Well, regardless of your age, doctors and scientists almost all agree that there are some things a geezer can do to keep hanging around in the best possible shape. Here they are:

"Your skin is enlarged."

LOSE THOSE POUNDS!

The typical American male today is 5 feet 9.5 inches and weighs an average of 191 pounds, giving him an average body mass index of 28.2. In other words, the average guy—and the average geezer—is overweight! Even if you're just average, you need to knock off about 10 pounds.

Hint: If your wife (assuming you still have one) goes on a diet, you will also automatically lose weight yourself.

Caveat: Suggesting that your wife go on a diet could lead to an ugly divorce or result in an early death—yours.

*"Of course, you see everything
from a very special perspective."*

DON'T DRINK SO MUCH!

This is a tough one—but it can be done. Don't drink before 5:00 P.M. except on rare occasions. Keep the booze out of sight. Stay away from bars. Switch to light beers. Volunteer once in a while to be the designated driver.

Hint: If you can't remember what you did yesterday, you're probably drinking too much.

Caveat: On the other hand, it may just be that you didn't do anything yesterday worth remembering.

QUIT SMOKING!

Another tough one. As W.C. Fields said—"It's easy—I've done it hundreds of times." First try willpower. Throw all those cigarettes out. Remind yourself they're called "coffin nails."

Hint: Think of all the money you would save if you didn't smoke.

Caveat: Maybe you could use the money you save to fumigate your clothes and your house.

GEEZER WORDS FOR DYING

- Kicking the bucket
- Assuming room temperature
- Turning up your toes
- Breathing your last
- Cashing it in
- Buying the farm
- Crossing the bar
- Popping off
- Giving up the ghost
- Taking the big nap
- Meeting the maker

"I try to eat right, but huge chunks of raw meat are all you find these days."

EAT BETTER

Face it—this means fruits and veggies. Some experts say you should eat five a day. That sounds a bit over the top—but vegetables aren't so bad if you skip Brussels sprouts and lima beans.

Hint: Some experts say red wine is really good for you.

Caveat: Let's hope that they were sober when they came to that conclusion.

*"Ah, Mr. Bremley. Nice to put
a face on a disease."*

MAKE A DATE WITH THE DOC

It pays to have a regular check-up—especially for geezers
whose bodies are in the throes of deterioration. Experts agree
on at least a once-a-year date with the doc. There's nothing
like having the doctor tell you you're likely to have a few more
birthdays in your future!

Hint: It might be worthwhile having a goal of trying to
outlive your doctor.

Caveat: Unless, of course, you have a really, really old
doctor.

AND OF COURSE...

Geezers everywhere can be grateful for the advances in science, medicine, pharmacology, and cosmetology that permit them to challenge the passing of the years. In fact, putting some of these advances together we can for the first time, envision the possibility of...

THE ARTIFICIAL GEEZER

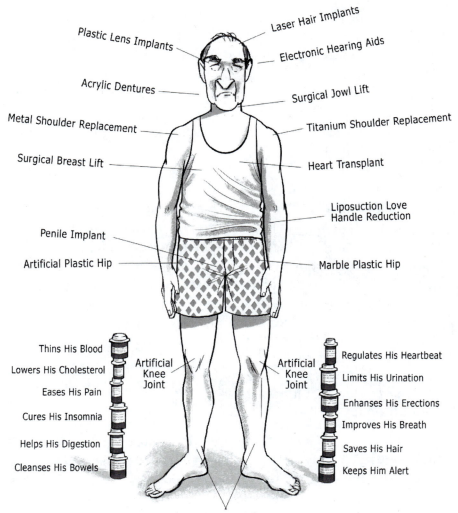

Laser Hair Implants

Plastic Lens Implants

Electronic Hearing Aids

Acrylic Dentures

Surgical Jowl Lift

Metal Shoulder Replacement

Titanium Shoulder Replacement

Surgical Breast Lift

Heart Transplant

Liposuction Love
Handle Reduction

Penile Implant

Artificial Plastic Hip

Marble Plastic Hip

Thins His Blood

Lowers His Cholesterol

Eases His Pain

Cures His Insomnia

Helps His Digestion

Cleanses His Bowels

Artificial
Knee
Joint

Artificial
Knee
Joint

Regulates His Heartbeat

Limits His Urination

Enhanses His Erections

Improves His Breath

Saves His Hair

Keeps Him Alert

Metal Ankle Replacements

HOW OLD IS OLD?

Geezers—like people of all kinds—are living longer than ever. The great miracle of the 20th century was the almost doubling of the human life span in the developed countries of the world.

You've probably heard the expression—"70 is now the new 50"—"80 is the now the new 70." Well it may not be too long before you will hear that "90 is the new 75"—or even "100 is the new 80"!

Sounds great, doesn't it? There you are at 100 or so, on a cruise in the South Pacific, playing shuffle-board on the deck, dispensing wisdom in the bar, and ogling the babes at the swimming pool.

A GEEZER TALE ABOUT LONGEVITY

A 100-year-old geezer and his wife stood before a judge asking that their divorce should be declared final. The judge said, "I'm going to grant this divorce, but first I must ask you why you waited so long." Replied the geezer, "We thought we should wait until the kids died."

Well, maybe. But picture this. You're 100 or so, sitting in a wheelchair, barely able to hold your head up, toothless and hard of hearing, looking out on a blurred and fuzzy world. You're living in a "home" where you have been stashed by your loved ones who wonder how long you're going to hang on, keeping them from getting their hands on your money.

How old is old? There's good reason to believe that "old" doesn't really settle in a guy until he loses his sense of joy and his lust for living. You're only old as you feel. It's not how many years that counts, it's what you do with your years. Or something like that. Whatever.

"Harmon was shaving and his stomach fell into the sink."

CHAPTER TEN

GEEZER-CISES
(The Way for Geezers to Exercise)

Now THERE WAS something else we need going to talk about. That's right, it's...exercise.

Unfortunately, the true geezer is just not into exercise. As Robert Hutchins, the long time president of the Chicago University, put it: "Occasionally, the urge to exercise comes over me, but I always lie down until it passes."

However, there's no denying that exercise is good for everyone—even for geezers. Now, we're not talking about those new terrifying places where young cardio-bots go to pummel themselves on machines. Horrors! These are nothing more than exercise boot camps, with people tethered to machines by digital monitors, their eyes glued to the banks of television sets, their ears covered by iPods, their legs frantically pumping up and down on mechanically simulated staircases. The thought of it is enough to give a geezer nightmares! No, that's not what we mean when we say geezers need exercise. We're talking instead about ...

GEEZER-CISES

"Be honest—how much are you exercising?"

"NO PAIN, NO GAIN"

NO WAY! That's the proper geezer reply to the old shibboleth that you have to torture yourself in order to get your body into better shape. And the geezer would be right, according to the latest theories. Experts now believe there is no reason to physically abuse your body when you are getting your exercise—and that it can actually be harmful—as if any geezer needed to be told that!

So that leaves. . .

Some other ways for geezers to get their exercise. Here are just a few:

"Now, don't get too excited—it could just be a hand puppet."

WALKING THE DOG

Ideal for daily geezer exercise, combining coordinated movement of all four limbs. Can also build upper arm strength if the accompanying dog strains at the leash. ***Downside risk:*** The embarrassment and humility of scooping the poop.

"I have a couple of other projects I'm excited about."

KICKING THE CAT

Usually a sudden response to an outrageous feline activity. Can build upper leg muscle while, at the same time, testing a geezer's balance. ***Downside risk:*** Missing the cat and spraining a ligament.

"Even my childhood dreams were of tax cuts."

GETTING OUT OF A CHAIR UNASSISTED

When a geezer is sunk deep in an easy chair, this can be a challenging exercise, requiring both strength and balance. Geezer must lean forward, push up with both arms and thrust legs straight. ***Downside risk:*** Being subject to ridicule if the first two or three attempts fail.

"The ball, I presume, is me."

GOLFING

Can involve up to 120 arm swings in just four hours, thereby inflicting a degree of exercise that would be intolerable in any other guise or circumstance. Can be repeated two or three times a week. ***Downside risk:*** Divorce.

"Nobody likes a showoff."

CATCHING A FISH

Not actually a competitive sport (the fish never wins), fishing can nevertheless be an exhausting three-stage exercise: putting on all the gear, hauling the equipment to the lake, and then the actual act of fishing. ***Downside risk:*** Drowning.

"Oh, so you wanna play rough, huh?"

SHUFFLEBOARDING

A traditional geezer exercise, usually undertaken in the company of other geezers or old biddies. Shuffleboarding exercises both legs but only one arm. ***Downside risk:*** Can result in health-endangering arguments as to whether a disk is on or near a line.

*"That's just wonderful, Filbert.
But don't expect me to get you off the floor."*

Cartoon by Clark Tate

STRETCHING

An excellent exercise for loosening up tight muscles and ancient bones. Also involves the severe athletic maneuver of going from a standing to a prone position. ***Downside risk:*** The possibility of having to beg for help in order to get up.

WORKING THE REMOTE

A superb exercise for preserving and even enhancing hand-eye coordination (or is it eye-hand coordination?). Also builds thumb dexterity and grip firmness. ***Downside risk:*** The likelihood of inflaming the passions of fellow viewers if over-used.

AND NOW FOR THE REALLY GOOD NEWS...

And the good news is that while a geezer is indulging in even mundane activities, he is actually burning up calories. Here are some exercise/calorie numbers worth remembering.

HOW A GEEZER CAN EXERCISE AND LOSE WEIGHT AT THE SAME TIME

Exercise	Calories Expended (per hour)
Walking into town	135
Washing and blow-drying a dog	185
Mowing the lawn	310
Plucking an ostrich	180
Playing chess	75
Spanking a grandchild	120
Butchering a steer	235
Shoveling the sidewalk	410
Riding a bike downhill	30
Riding a bike uphill	240
Giving a neighbor the finger	14
Swinging a cat	120
Demolishing a computer	217
Stoning a prostitute	185
Screaming at a kid	25

THE FINE ART OF BEING IDLE

As a postscript to this exhausting chapter on exercise, it should be pointed out that some people believe that the real secret of life is to do as little as possible, to say nothing of deliberately exercising. There is, in fact, an entire book on this subject—*How To Be Idle*—written by a writer/philosopher named Tom Hodgkinson. Hodgkinson is the founder of a British magazine called *The Idler,* which devotes its pages to various methods by which a person can do nothing. He advocates the banning of alarm clocks, lying in bed in the morning, having long leisurely lunches, and afternoon naps which blend seamlessly into extensive and relaxing cocktail hours and late dinners.

This is an exciting alternative for geezers, of course. But Hodgkinson would be more convincing if he had not gone to the hard work of writing 286 pages to get his idea across!

"That will be the gold standard by which all other naps are judged."

"Whistle, you dumb bastard!"

—

CHAPTER ELEVEN

GEEZER SEX

(A Complete Review of Great Geezer Sex)

. . . . .
Geezer Sex
. . . . .

"I should have bought more crap."

CHAPTER TWELVE

GEEZER POSSESSIONS
(What It Takes to Lead the Geezer Lifestyle)

OVER THE DECADES the average geezer will have accumulated a treasure trove of possessions—or, to put it another way, a junk yard's worth of stuff! The main reason for this is that *most geezers never throw anything away.*

GEEZER STUFF

Consider a typical geezer wardrobe:

	Geezer Owns	Geezer Wears
TIES	37	4
SHIRTS	15	2
SHOES (pairs)	8	1
SOCKS (pairs)	16	3
SWEATERS	9	2
JACKETS	6	1
SUITS	6	0

So why is this geezer's closet stuffed with all those things he never wears? In all likelihood, there are valid reasons. Each of the ties he doesn't wear probably has some meaning in his life. For instance, that blue stripped tie might be the one he was wearing when he closed that big deal in 1973. And that ghastly red tie is the one his wife really hates.

And even though he doesn't wear suits any more, he has to keep all of them because he can't make up his mind which suit he wants to be buried in.

But mostly he keeps all that stuff because he can't seem to find the time to get rid of it. He just never gets around to it. So he has lots of stuff.

Different geezers, of course, have different kinds of stuff. Intellectual geezers have lots of books (some of which they have actually read). Golfing geezers have closets and garages filled with old clubs and souvenir golf balls. Gardening geezers have racks of gardening clothes, pairs of old pants, hats and sun visors. The fishing geezer has a basement filled with rods, poles and hip boots—drawers full of various hooks and fly ties.

There are, however, several things that all geezers—regardless of profession or past-time, should own. Think of these as "geezer stuff in common." Let's examine a few.

"You know, Marion, one of the things that have stood the test of time is these tassel oxfords."

THE CANE

Every geezer, even geezers with strong limbs, healthy hips and splendid knees, should own and, whenever possible, carry a cane. The practical uses of a cane in the hands of a geezer are numerous. But in addition to that there is the element of *character* that a cane imparts to a geezer. "Here," a cane says, "is a man who has *lived* and *suffered*—a man who won't give up—a man who strives on in the face of adversity."

Any cane is preferable to no cane. But not every cane sends out the right message. Consider the following non-geezer-appropriate canes.

TEN THINGS A GEEZER CAN DO WITH A CANE

1. Pound the ground for emphasis.
2. Point and shake to signal anger.
3. Wave to a friend.
4. Chop in the air to threaten violence.
5. Trip a passerby.
6. Slug a rival.
7. Summon a cab.
8. Thwak a dog.
9. Slug a cat.
10. Assist with walking.

THE FOUR-LEGGED CANE

Too medicinal. Indicates serious infirmity on the part of the geezer—makes geezer look old and unwell. Could invite unwelcome sympathy.

THE FANCY-KNOB CANE

Too pretentious. Makes a geezer look stuffy. Also has no real grip for mounting assaults, or for defending against dog attacks.

THE METAL CANE

Much too institutional. Implies that the cane was bought with a prescription—rather than selected for personal enjoyment.

THE GNARLED CANE

Too showy. Connotes that the owner is sort of an exhibitionist—cares too much about appearance and impressing others.

THE LIGHT COLORED CANE

Watch it. People will think you're blind or do not see clearly. Geezers don't want to be helped, for God's sake.

THE SOUVENIR CANE

Pathetic. Covered with emblems of a world's fair or a city or an event. Implies you think being somewhere was a big deal.

None of the previous canes is really geezer friendly, nor do any of them send the right geezer message. On the following page is pictured the ideal cane for the true geezer.

THE PLAIN, SIMPLE, BLACK OR BROWN CURVED-HANDLED CANE WITH SIGNS OF LONG USE

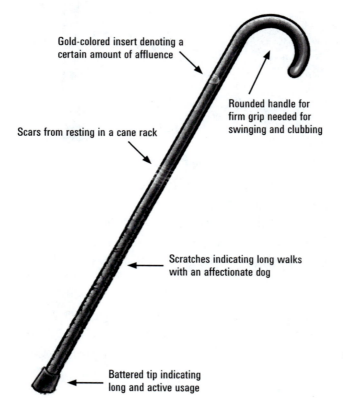

Gold-colored insert denoting a certain amount of affluence

Rounded handle for firm grip needed for swinging and clubbing

Scars from resting in a cane rack

Scratches indicating long walks with an affectionate dog

Battered tip indicating long and active usage

Here is the perfect geezer cane. Strong, sturdy, unpretentious, traditional and masculine. Also perfectly styled for flaying at animals, threatening small children and for the other many uses to which a geezer cane can be put (see the list on page 129).

THE DOG

A great many geezers have a dog—their *own* dog. Not just a family pet, but a dog answerable only to the geezer himself. There are several reasons a geezer might want such a dog:

1. Dogs can't talk back
2. Dogs aren't always telling you what to do
3. Dogs aren't after your money.

Of course, not every dog is an ideal geezer dog. If a dog is too small, for instance, a geezer could trip over it and break a hip. And if a dog is too big, there is always a chance that it could jump up on a geezer, knock him down, and cause him to—yes, break a hip.

According to the *Illustrated Encyclopedia of Dogs* there are more than a thousand different recognized breeds of *canis familiarius*. So a geezer has a truly baffling job in selecting the exact and perfect pooch to serve his needs. To make the task easier, here are some of the dog breeds that are *not* suitable for the geezer.

"They were bred originally to be hors d'oeuvres."

THE CHIHUAHUA
Much too small. Dinky, in fact. Too easily stumbled over, too difficult to find on dark days. Too "yappie."

THE TOY ANYTHING
Unmanly. Any dog that has "toy" in its name is unsuitable. Could easily be mistaken for a cat.

THE SAINT BERNARD
Too big. With a single leap it could put a geezer in the hospital. Redeeming feature: Sometimes comes with brandy around its neck.

THE PIT BULL
Heaven forbid! Far too intimidating. Most geezers couldn't even sleep well with one of these in the house. Even scary to look at!

THE YORKSHIRE TERRIER

Too fancy. No geezer wants a dog that thinks it's better than he is. Might not be willing to walk with a geezer.

THE LHASA APSO

The what? No geezer wants to have a dog that can't see. Redeeming feature: could double as a mop.

THE POLISH SHEEPDOG

Too absurd. Also too high maintenance. The real geezer does not want to spend more time grooming his dog than he does grooming himself.

THE GREYHOUND

Too fast. No geezer can keep up with a dog built for such speed. On long walks, the average geezer could drop dead from exhaustion.

THE BLOODHOUND

Has too keen a sense of smell. No geezer wants a dog that looks at him disdainfully from clear across the room.

THE DACHSHUND

Looks like a doorstop. Also seriously short of legs, sometimes forcing a geezer to drag it on long walks.

Having thus simplified the matter of dog selection for any geezer by eliminating these unsuitable breeds, we now offer the best of all dogs for full geezer pleasure and enjoyment.

THE LOVABLE MUTT

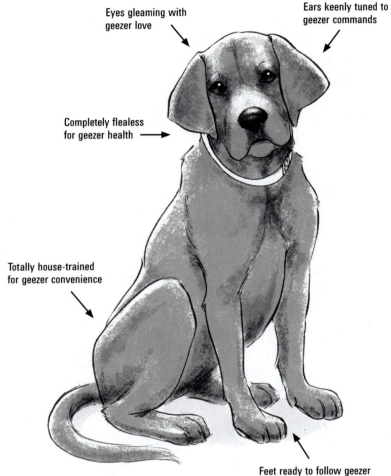

Eyes gleaming with geezer love

Ears keenly tuned to geezer commands

Completely flealess for geezer health

Totally house-trained for geezer convenience

Feet ready to follow geezer on a moment's notice

This is not to say that there are not other kinds of dogs that can bring joy into a geezer's life. But a dog without breeding, bloodlines or pedigree can come into a geezer's life without pretentions—without an agenda of its own. He comes "geezer-friendly" and ready to serve and love!

THE CHAIR

Every geezer needs his own chair—a chair that is positioned exactly where he wants it (usually in front of the television set)—a chair that no one else dares to sit in. As with so many other geezer possessions, not any chair is suitable. Selection of the geezer chair is usually made over a long period of time—trial and error—before the perfect chair is found. Once proclaimed and once positioned, it should never be changed, never be moved, and never violated by the presence of another body.

Some chairs, of course, are never appropriate for the true geezer. In order to simplify the choice for any geezer still looking for his perfect lifetime chair, we cite the following chair styles that should *not* be considered.

WHAT REAL GEEZERS CARRY IN THEIR WALLETS (IN DESCENDING ORDER OF IMPORTANCE)

Driver's License
Money
Medicare card
Medicare "Plan D" card
Credit Cards
AARP Membership Card
Photos of Grandchildren
Business Cards
List of Phone Numbers
Photo of Spouse

THE FRENCH CHAIR

Too foreign. A geezer needs an all-American chair. Looks like an ideal chair for your pretentious maiden aunt.

THE WICKER CHAIR

Looks comfortable—but has certain drawbacks for the geezer. Among them is the serious danger of splinters.

THE ARTSY-FARTSY CHAIR

A chair only a crafts fair could love. Probably carved from a single piece of hard wood. A work of art does not a chair make.

THE BIZARRE CHAIR

No geezer wants to put up with a chair that looks this weird and this uncomfortable. Especially if it looks as if it's made up of—say, giant hot dogs.

THE DESIGNER CHAIR
Looks as if there were three designers involved—and they all got their way. Could give a geezer nightmares.

THE BARE BONES CHAIR
Not a chance. Five minutes in this chair and the average geezer would be sore as a boil and stiff as a board. Ouch!

THE CONFUSED CHAIR
Some chairs can't make up their minds whether to be a chair, a couch or a settee. A geezer wouldn't know where to put his head or his butt!

THE HARD LEATHER CHAIR
Close but no cigar. Looks hard as a rock and about as comfortable. A geezer leaning back too fast could get a concussion.

Having eliminated these kinds of chairs, it is now easier to recommend the "ideal" geezer chair.

THE OVER-STUFFED, LEATHER, FULL-ARMED CHAIR

Back ready to receive geezer's head as he slumps in chair

Chair arms that permit geezer's arms to either rest or hang over the side

Seat cushion shaped to fit contours of geezer's butt

There are a number of manufacturers that make this style of geezer chair. A meticulous search of catalogues and chair stores should turn up a good "geezer chair." But remember, once found, it might not be ideal until it has been used for years—even decades—and until it has fully adapted itself to the weight, body and contours of the owner. Patience and understanding are recommended.

THE CAR

Every geezer, from cradle to grave, spends a good part of his life on wheels. And during his prime geezer years he needs a proper car. Of course, he also needs a driver's license to enable him to use the car. Mobility is of prime importance to the true geezer because he would otherwise have to depend on others to get about, and this might make it necessary to be nice to them.

The Wheels of Life

As with other important geezer possessions, of course, not any car will do. Selection of the proper car can have a great and positive impact on a geezer's life. Selection of the *wrong* car can affect a geezer's life adversely.

The following information is offered as a general geezer guide to car ownership—and the cars a true geezer will want to avoid.

THE LAMBORGHINI

Much too fancy and much too foreign. Also much too expensive. Fortunately, most geezers can't even pronounce "Lamborghini."

THE ROLLS-ROYCE

Too aristocratic and show-offy. Most geezers are down-to-earth guys. The very idea of a Rolls seems contrary to the "geezer mystique."

THE HUMMER

Huge, boxy, warlike—more suited to battle than motoring. Tank-like, it might remind some geezers of their war service.

THE CONVERTIBLE

Too breezy. Geezer drivers would be likely to catch cold. Also at high speeds a "comb-over" would flap in the wind.

THE SUB-COMPACT

"Sub" means small. "Compact" means small. So this car is "smaller than small." Most geezers could get in, but it might take the "jaws of life" to get them out.

THE VOLVO

Too foreign. Made in some faraway place—God knows where! Also, no self-respecting geezer wants to own a car with a name that sounds like a female body part.

THE HYBRID

Doesn't even sound good—neither this nor that. Geezers like clear decisions, not muddled compromises. And they like a car that *sounds* like a car!

THE S.U.V.

Most geezers don't even know what S.U.V. stands for—let alone what kind of car it is. Or is it a car? Heaven only knows. Maybe it's a truck, for heaven's sake!

To find the kind of car a geezer should own—the kind of car a geezer can truly love—look at the next page...

THE TEN-YEAR-OLD BUICK ROADMASTER SEDAN

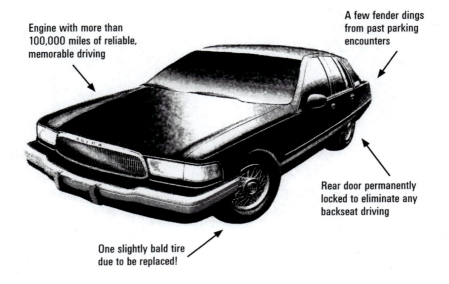

Engine with more than 100,000 miles of reliable, memorable driving

A few fender dings from past parking encounters

Rear door permanently locked to eliminate any backseat driving

One slightly bald tire due to be replaced!

Now here is a car that any geezer could love—big, comfortable, unpretentious, and road-tested. It's been a great car for the first 100,000 miles—so there is no reason why it shouldn't be great for the next 100,000 miles! A real geezer gets it serviced whenever it sounds as if it's falling apart. Also, every geezer car should give his car a name—like "The Blue Bomber" or "The Red Hustler" or "The Intimidator." This indicates the car's long and loving relationship with the geezer.

Now let's consider just a few things that no self-respecting geezer will ever buy, ever own, or ever attempt to use.

THE CELL PHONE

Doesn't like talking on the phone even when he's at home. Can't imagine *never* getting away from the telephone.

THE COMPUTER

Wonders if E-mail is anything like "V" mail. Has no desire to get boring messages from people he hardly knows.

THE IPOD

Most geezers assume that anyone who has a button in his ear is wearing a hearing aid.

Rule number one for any geezer
buying any appliance of any kind:

DON'T BUY IT UNLESS IT HAS
AN "ON" AND "OFF" BUTTON!

Anyone selecting a *gift* for a geezer should keep the following overall guide in mind: These words describe what a geezer might like—or not like:

BAD	GOOD
New-fangled	Old fashioned
Experimental	Tried & True
Innovative	Proven
Cutting edge	Traditional
Exciting	Comfortable
The latest	Time-tested
Novel	Venerable
Modern	Seasoned

And no matter what a geezer might own—no matter how lengthy his list of possessions might be—it's not complete unless he has that most prized possession of all—

A ROOM OF HIS OWN!

This is the space that the true geezer refers to as his "sanctum-sactorium." It is the place of refuge to which he flees to escape the cares of the day, the demands of his friends and the noise of his family. Here he is surrounded by all his favorite things and they provide an environment in which he can truly "bliss out." This is where he feels safe!

The geezer's wife refers to this as his "pouting room." She and a few others are sometimes permitted to enter, but only under certain conditions: a.) they can't change the television channel, b.) they can't fuss with the thermostat, and c.) they can't rearrange things. The cleaning lady sometimes comes in to vacuum the floor and to dust. But woe to her or anyone else who tries to "straighten things up."

THE GREAT GEEZER LAIR

1. Curtain drawn to eliminate prying eyes.
2. Fully stocked liquor cabinet.
3. Photos of family members, none of them recent.
4. Plaques signifying membership in Rotary, Elks and VFW.
5. VHS cassette player (he doesn't even know about DVDs yet).
6. Tapes, including *Casablanca, The Dirty Dozen,* and ten Clint Eastwood films.
7. Remotes for TV and tape player.
8. Large television set, now five years old.
9. Fireplace, lighted only for major events or holidays.
10. The place where the computer would be if he owned one.
11. A jumble of old magazines and current newspapers.
12. The first dollar he ever earned, framed.
13. Library shelves with books including *The Big Book of Revenge, A Perfect Mess, Feel Younger Every Year, The Memory Manual,* and *The Complete Geezer Guidebook.*
14. Tribute given him at his retirement party, which he can barely remember.
15. THE CHAIR!

And now...

A MAGAZINE IDEA FOR A VERY SPECIAL MARKET

"George Stoner is here from Terre Haute.
He and Henry are talking over old times."

CHAPTER THIRTEEN

WHERE GEEZERS GATHER
(Places Where Geezers Meet to Eat and Greet)

G EEZERS ARE BASICALLY NOT clustering creatures. Many prefer solitude over the company of others. But even geezers get lonely on occasion—and venture out in search of company, often the company of fellow geezers.

Following is a brief and informal listing of geezer habitats—where geezers can be found, if not in abundance, at least in limited groupings. It is offered not as a definitive geezer gazetteer, but merely as a helpful guide to those in search of geezer sightings.

	AT HOME	AT PLAY	AT TABLE	AT THE BAR
New York, NY	**Carnegie East House** Geezers guaranteed at 95th and 2nd Avenue. More than 100 seniors on hand at any given time in various stages of dilapidation.	**Washington Square** Where geezers play chess and checkers for fun and high stakes while catching the sunshine.	**La Cote Basque** Upscale dining for the mature crowd including geezer gourmets.	**McSorley's Old Ale House** 150 year old saloon in lower East Side. Geezer friendly from front to back. Only recently allowed women.
Sun City, AR	Almost Anywhere	Almost Anywhere	Almost Anywhere	Almost Anywhere
Dallas, TX	**Pegasus Villas** An adult community that is a "geezer haven." Everything to keep a geezer quiet and contented.	**Old City Park** Surrounded by historic homes. A trip back in time for geezers who like to reminisce.	**Local** Great name for an old neighborhood eatery. Housed in the historic Boyd Hotel. Geezers feel right at home here.	**Double Wide Bar** Great "trailer trash" décor. Cheap beer and terrific atmosphere. Fun for geezers.
Sun City, FL	Almost Anywhere	Almost Anywhere	Almost Anywhere	Almost Anywhere
Seattle, WA	**Ballard Manor** Geezers running amok in relative luxury and with all the services.	**Pike St.** On the waterfront with all kinds of geezer action. Geezers should beware of flying fish.	**Garage** Housed in an old auto repair garage. Geezers feel right at home. Comes with its own pool hall.	**Monkey Pub** A haven for the mature crowd as well as the hippies. Old fashioned juke box adds charm.
Sun City, CA	Almost Anywhere	Almost Anywhere	Almost Anywhere	Almost Anywhere
San Francisco, CA	**The Towers** Where wealthy geezers are outnumbered only by rich old biddies.	**Portsmouth Square** Geezers at chess, checkers and conversation. Tourist geezers a plus.	**Tadich Grille** Old time eatery with lots of old-time customers. Excellent geezer sightings.	**Original Joe's** Traditional bar with geezer stools waiting for old customers. A geezer tradition.
Holiday City, NC	Almost Anywhere	Almost Anywhere	Almost Anywhere	Almost Anywhere

	AT HOME	AT PLAY	AT TABLE	AT THE BAR
Chicago, IL	**Bell Plain Commons** Upscale living for the "mature" crowd. Great place to meet and greet some old timers.	**Wrigley Field** Best ball park in America. Cozy and noisy. Great place for geezers to see the Cubs lose.	**Harry Carry's** Named after the venerable geezer announcer. Good food and slow service make it "geezer perfect."	**Burwood Tap** A family-run bar since 1933. Definitely geezer friendly. Features backgammon games.
Pinehurst, NC	Almost Anywhere	Almost Anywhere	Almost Anywhere	Almost Anywhere
Boston, MA	**Hale House** On Marlborough St. An elderly folks' home with lots of activities for geezers and their mates.	**Copley Square Park** Nice place to chill and take in the city. Lots of benches for geezers to rest and relax.	**Locke-Ober** Oldest upscale restaurant in Boston. Only geezers with deep pockets dine here.	**Harp Irish Pub** Best of the old sod pubs. Irish geezers often in attendance for health reasons.
Venice, FL	Almost Anywhere	Almost Anywhere	Almost Anywhere	Almost Anywhere
Atlanta, GA	**The Atrium** At Georgetown Park. Lively center for feverish geezer activity. All the good stuff.	**Turner Park** Where the Braves play. Named after Terrible Ted. Look for geezers in the stands.	**Hal's** On the "dead end" side of Old Ivy. Great local haunt. Slightly cramped room brings geezers closer together.	**Manuel's Tavern** Atlanta's quintessential bar. Almost a museum. Geezers in regular attendance.
Sedona, AR	Almost Anywhere	Almost Anywhere	Almost Anywhere	Almost Anywhere
Carmel, CA	**The Manor** Mostly rich geezers at this distinguished and sought-after senior residence.	**Old Capital Club** In Monterey, this upscale men's club is affectionately known as "God's waiting room."	**Club XIX** At The Lodge in Pebble Beach. One or two geezers guaranteed at all times.	**Hog's Breath** If Clint Eastwood shows up, you're guaranteed at least one geezer!
Hot Springs Village, AR	Almost Anywhere	Almost Anywhere	Almost Anywhere	Almost Anywhere

	AT HOME	AT PLAY	AT TABLE	AT THE BAR
Philadelphia, PA	**Fountains** At Logan Square. A retirement community worthy of the name. Geezers in abundance.	**Arch St. Meetinghouse** Largest Friends meeting place in this world. Exhibits and tours—some led by real geezers.	**Bookbinders** The old and original—more than 100 years old. Certainly old enough for geezers to feel at home.	**McGillin Old Ale House** Oldest bar in the city. Located in a picturesque alley. But doesn't serve Guinness—even to geezers.
Venice, FL	Almost Anywhere	Almost Anywhere	Almost Anywhere	Almost Anywhere
Washington, DC	**The Capital of the United States** This is where the Senators live and work. Just go to the Senate chamber and you'll see more geezers than you can count.	**The Mall** Yes, lots of kids and families, but you're also assured of geezers— especially at the WWII Memorial.	**1789** This restaurant looks as old as its name. And it's in the oldest part of town. Good food—and geezers are guaranteed!	**Old Ebbets Grill** Watering hole of veteran pols of all hues and ages. And it's right across from the White House.
Miami Beach, FL	Almost Anywhere	Almost Anywhere	Almost Anywhere	Almost Anywhere

"Buzz off, Louise! That was only till death us did part."

CHAPTER FOURTEEN

GREAT GEEZER GAGS
(Geezers Can Be the Funniest People!)

JOKES ABOUT GEEZERS abound. For some reason, geezers seem to lend themselves to humorous tales—almost as if there was something intrinsically funny about being a geezer. There is little geezers can do about this, so they might as well join the fun and laugh along with everyone else. Following are a dozen or so "geezer gags" that give everyone—regardless of age or disposition—a chuckle or two.

GEEZER STORY NO. 1

A disheveled old geezer hadn't been to see his doctor in years, and simply refused to go. Finally his wife made an appointment for him, threw him in the car, drove him to the doctor's office and dragged him into the examining room. The doctor came in, consulted his medical record, and said, "For starters, I'm going to need a urine sample, a stool sample and a blood sample." The geezer, somewhat hard of hearing, turned to his wife and asked, "What did he say?" His wife replied sharply, "The doctor said that you should give him your shorts!"

GEEZER STORY NO. 2

A geezer signed up for a round of golf, but explained to the pro that his vision was very poor. The pro, in a burst of inspiration, paired him up with another geezer who had excellent vision. On the first tee, the first geezer hit the ball, then turned to the other and said, "Did you see where it went?" "Yes," said geezer number two. "Excellent," said the first, "where did it go?" Replied the second geezer, "I forgot."

GEEZER STORY NO. 3

An old geezer at a fashion show, admiring the models as they paraded past, said to his companion, "When I look at these beautiful girls, I wish I was twenty years older." His friend said, "Surely, you mean twenty years younger." Replied the geezer, "No, I mean twenty years older. Then I wouldn't give a damn."

GEEZER STORY NO. 4

A geezer, celebrating his golden wedding anniversary, was visited that evening by a fairy who said she would grant him one wish. The geezer whispered quietly to the fairy that he really wished he was married to someone thirty years younger. When he awoke in the morning, he found that his wish had come true. He was 105 years old!

GEEZER STORY NO. 5

A geezer was extremely ill and in danger of dying. A priest was called, administered the last rites, and then asked, "Do you denounce Satan and all his works?" The geezer remained silent. "Why don't you answer," the priest demanded. "Listen," said the geezer, "at this point I'm not going to antagonize anybody!"

GEEZER STORY NO. 6

A shaky old geezer was being examined by a doctor, who noted his trembling hands. "Do you drink too much, do you think?" the doctor asked. "Not anymore," said the geezer. "Lately I spill most of it!"

GEEZER STORY NO. 7

A geezer got up at a banquet celebrating his eightieth birthday, and placed this watch on the rostrum, announcing, "I want to make sure I don't talk too long, so I will occasionally glance at my watch." He then proceeded to talk at great length about his life and times—and droned on and on. Finally, someone in the audience yelled, "Forget the watch—there's a calendar on the wall!"

GEEZER STORY NO. 8

A geezer showed up at his dentist's office, accompanied by his wife. He immediately said to the dentist, "There's a tooth that needs to be extracted, but I don't want you to use any pain killer because I have a date to play golf and I know that stuff takes a long time—so I want you to just yank it out." "You mean" said the dentist, "without any Novocain or gas? That's going to be extremely painful." "I know," said the geezer, "but I'm in a real hurry." "All right," replied the dentist. "Which tooth is it?" Said the geezer, "Get up in the chair, dear, and show the dentist which one it is."

GEEZER STORY NO. 9

A geezer's young wife, after a romantic dinner, said to her husband, "Let's go upstairs and make love." "Make up your mind," said the geezer, "I can't do both."

GEEZER STORY NO. 10

Two geezers met in the hallway of a retirement home, and after a brief conversation, one of them said, "What on earth is that in your ear?" The second geezer removed it, looked at it and replied, "Good Lord, it's a suppository." The other geezer thought for a moment and then responded—"I hate to ask where your hearing aid is!"

GEEZER STORY NO. 11

A geezer, chatting with a friend, said, "My wife and I went to a really wonderful restaurant last night." "What restaurant was it?" asked the friend.

The geezer looked puzzled for a moment, then brightened and said, "What's the name of that flower that women like to get. The one that has red petals and a thorny stem?"

"You mean a rose?"

"Yes, that's it," said the geezer, as he got out of his chair, walked to the door of the other room, and yelled, "Rose! What's the name of that restaurant we ate in last night?"

GEEZER STORY NO. 12

A geezer moved into a retirement home, and at breakfast the following morning he was joined by a long-time resident lady. "You're new here, aren't you?" she inquired. "Yes," replied the geezer. "Where were you before you came here?"

she asked. "In prison," he said. "I was serving twenty years for murdering my wife." The lady brightened considerably and said, "So you're *single!*"

GEEZER STORY NO. 13

A geezer, facing serious surgery, requested that the operation be performed by his own son, who was a skilled surgeon. The request, though unusual, was honored. On the day of the surgery, just before the anesthesia was administered, the geezer looked up at his son and said, "I think you should know, son, that if I die, your mother plans to come and live with you."

GEEZER STORY NO. 14

Three geezers were chatting in the lobby of their retirement home, commiserating with each other about their ailments.

One said, "My arms are so weak I can hardly hold up my coffee cup."

Another said, "My eyesight is so bad I missed the cup when I poured my coffee."

A third said, "My neck is so stiff I couldn't even turn my head to see where the coffee was."

After a brief pause, one of them replied, "Let's stop complaining. We should all just be grateful we can still drive."

CHAPTER FIFTEEN

WHEN GEEZERS BECOME EXPENDABLE
(What to Do When the Clock Winds Down)

A LL GEEZERS ARE, by definition, old. The problem is that they then become even older. Eventually their doctors—to say nothing of their heirs—begin to wonder how long they're going to stick around. At some point, geezers become regarded as, well, expendable! Some cultures are more direct than others about dispatching the elderly.

"Hold it—we almost forgot his benefits package."

But even in our society, the warning signs are clear:

1. Being described as "spry," "chipper," or that worst of all adjectives, "alert."
2. Hearing people discuss you as if you weren't there. "Is that something he should eat?" "Did he have a hat?"
3. An inordinate interest in the terms of your will, your power of attorney or your living will.

Of course, you also know, in your heart of hearts, that somewhere along the line you are going to—as Shakespeare put it—"shuffle off this mortal coil." There are a few things you can do in the meantime to make your departure an effective and memorable event.

SPRUCE UP YOUR OBITUARY!

Let's assume that you have led a non-celebrity life—perhaps even a boring, humdrum life; certainly not the stuff of dazzling obituaries. Well, it's not too late to do something about that. Why should you?

Look at it this way. Within a few generations after you've gone, it is unlikely that there will be anyone living who actually remembers you. All that will be left will be your obituary—the official, recognized record of your ever having been on this planet. You want it to sound as good as possible.

Let's take a look at two obits:

John Smith died last Tuesday after a brief illness. Mr. Smith was a longtime citizen of Smallville, a member of the Kiwanis Club and the local Masonic Order. For forty years, he was a loyal employee of Acme Tool and Dye and its predecessor companies.

He is survived by his wife, Edna, and two children, Rose and Jacob. There will be no funeral service open to the public but contributions can be made to Friends of the Library.

Now consider this obituary:

John "Globetrotter" Smith died Tuesday after acquiring an unnamed disease on one of his recent foreign travels. Mr. Smith used Smallville as his base of operations in recent years and always claimed it as his favorite American city. Smith was celebrated for what was reputed to be the world's largest collection of Peruvian Indian blowguns. He was also a recognized authority on the cannibalistic customs of the pygmy tribes of ancient East Africa. Smith occupied managerial positions at Acme Tool and Dye for more than forty years, seeing that company through several international mergers. He is survived by his first wife, Edna, and his two recognized children, Rose

"I'd just like to live long enough to hear what people say about me when I'm dead, that's all."

and Jacob. A public funeral ceremony is planned to which both local and international guests are invited. Contributions should be made to the John Smith Foundation for the Betterment of the World's Indigenous Peoples.

Now, of course, these two obituaries are for the same gentleman. Yet the first portrays a man who has led a really routine, if not boring, life. The second sounds like the life of a man who *lived*—who led a life of excitement and derring-do.

Let's analyze, for a moment, the key elements of that second obit.

John "Globetrotter" Smith *(he gave himself that nickname in his last year and insisted that at least two friends call him that, which they did—sarcastically)* died Tuesday after acquiring an unnamed disease on one of his foreign travels *(he caught a cold in Windsor)*. Mr. Smith used Smallville as his base of operations *(that is, he lived there)* and claimed it as his favorite American city *(and about the only one he really knew!)*. Mr. Smith was celebrated *(by his wife)* for what was reputed to be *(by him)* the world's largest collection of Peruvian Indian blow guns *(he bought two on E-Bay, no one else has a collection)*. He was also a recognized authority *(by his wife again)* on the cannibalistic customs of the pygmy tribes of ancient East Africa *(he read about them once in the Encyclopedia Britannica)*. Smith occupied managerial positions at Acme Tool and Dye *(he once had an assistant for a couple of years)* for more than forty years and saw that company through several international mergers *(he had nothing to do with the mergers but he did "see them through.")* He is survived by his first wife, Edna *(and his only wife)*, and his two recognized children, Rose and Jacob *(the addition of "recognized" hints at his profligate love life)*. A public funeral ceremony is planned to which both local and international guests are invited *(why not?)*. Contributions should be made to the John Smith Foundation for the Betterment of the World's Indigenous Peoples *(a foundation he set up last month with $500. So far, it has only distributed one bottle of gin to an American Indian)*.

So you see what a little imagination, creativity and planning can accomplish. There's still time to spruce up *your* obit. Here are just a few things you might consider:

1. Give yourself a memorable nickname, such as "Ace" or "Whizzer."
2. Take up an exotic hobby—bee-keeping, llama raising, or the study of Indian pottery.
3. Plunge into charity work. "He was active in a number of local and national charities" ... has a really nice ring to it.
4. Send a small check to a museum or dance group. This makes you a "contributor to the arts."

And, above all, do not leave the writing of your obituary to strangers. Write it in advance yourself—and don't hesitate to be...well, creative. Your local newspaper has enough to do without checking every last fact in your little life story. So take a crack at it. Do your best. It's your last real chance at immortality!

FORGIVE YOUR ENEMIES! OR BETTER YET, GET EVEN WITH THE BASTARDS!

Think of all those people who've treated you badly over the years—owed you money—cheated you at the office—lied to you. The philosophers say that at this age it is time to forgive, to come to terms with your rivals and enemies. Real geezers, however, think forgiveness is for sissies. The real geezer wants his revenge!

Ramon Narvaez, a 19th century Spanish politician, set the right course on his deathbed: "I do not have to forgive my enemies," he said. "I have had them all shot!"

Now that's the spirit! Of course, most geezers don't have the ability—or perhaps even the willingness—to have their enemies and rivals shot. But if a geezer is more inclined toward revenge than reconciliation, then he needs some alternative means of getting even. Fortunately, help is at hand. It comes in the form of a remarkable book called *The Big Book of Revenge* by George Hayduke, which lists more than 200 ways of getting back at the people who have wronged you. Here are just a few of the more mundane tactics recommended.

1. Write a fake obituary of the detested one and send it to the local paper. With any luck, they'll run it, and the guy will spend years living it down.

2. In early January, run an ad saying the detested one is paying $10 apiece for old Christmas trees. Give the address, of course.

3. Call the detested one, posing as the electric company, and tell him his last check bounced. He'll spend at least a couple of hours trying to clear that up. Call him just before the close of business and he'll spend a sleepless night.

4. Send out a lot of fake change of address cards to the detested one's friends, club members and utility companies.

5. Let the air out of his car tires some night. Five minutes of effort on your part will cost him at least several hours of maddening work.
6. Run a small ad proclaiming a garage sale at his house starting at 6:00 A.M. on Sunday.
7. If the detested one is a neighbor with a fence, open the gate whenever you pass. There's no telling what might get out—or in!
8. Urinate in the driver-door lock of his car. It will rust out within just a few days

If any geezer finds these techniques a bit harsh, there are always gentler methods available. He could, for instance, *disinherit* them. Yes, that's right! Just because people you don't like never expected to get any funds at your demise doesn't mean that you can't specifically and emphatically get in one last insult by giving them *nothing* when your will is read. Think of the posthumous joy you could get when everyone discovers that you have *disinherited*:

- That guy your wife had an affair with years ago
- Your old boss who refused to give you a promotion when you really deserved it
- The paper boy who always left your paper out on the lawn when it was raining
- The neighbor with the barking dog (you could also disinherit the *dog* if you wanted to)
- The driver who dented your car fender in the parking lot, even though you don't know who he is
- All the telemarketers who have interrupted your dinner over the years
- That high school teacher who flunked you in phys. ed. just because you couldn't do the rope climb
- The president of the United States—the one who raised your taxes right after you voted for him

Or you might consider naming a detested one in your will, leaving him a lot of things you don't have—your yacht, your gold bullion, your foreign holdings. He could spend years trying to track them down.

So take your pick. Select your enemies carefully. Show some discretion in choosing your methods. But just think of all the peace of mind it could bring you to get even with all those rascals before time runs out—and maybe even after!

*"Now read me the part again
where I disinherit everybody."*

PLAN YOUR OWN FUNERAL

Why not! Celebrities do it. Former presidents do it. There's no reason you shouldn't make sure that things go exactly the way you want at your final farewell. Otherwise, you run the risk that they'll have one of those "celebration of life" things with everyone smiling, laughing, drinking and having a good time. No! You want sadness, weeping, even gnashing of teeth.

You're gone! It's a tragedy! You're going to be horribly, sickeningly missed! Things are never going to be the same. Let's have some tears! After all, there'll be plenty of time for smiles and feeling good later—*when the will is read!*

Here's a short list of things to do:

1. Designate that lots of money be spent on the casket. Otherwise, you're likely to be buried in an old box.
2. Select as pallbearers the most important people you've ever met. If they don't accept, name the most important people you actually know.
3. Designate your most eloquent and greatest admirers (or lacking these, your least articulate detractors) to give funeral orations.
4. Pick out the most mournful music imaginable to be played during the service, the kind that is certain to provoke tears and anguish.
5. Design your own headstone. Otherwise, you might get a cheap, ground-level cement block with just your name (possibly misspelled) and the date of your birth (estimated) and death (not estimated).
6. Arrange for a huge gratuity for the presiding preacher to make sure he doesn't give you the quick, throw-away service.
7. If all else fails, hire professional mourners!

Having thus assured yourself of an adequate send off, you need to have only one regret. As Garrison Keillor said, "They say such nice things about people at their funerals that it makes me sad to realize I'm going to miss mine—by just a few days."

THINK UP SOME GREAT "LAST WORDS!"

Don't find yourself at the last moment completely at a loss for immortal words— like Pancho Villa—whose departing words were, "Tell them I said something!"

You need to leave the world with something they'll talk about for years to come—a legacy they won't soon forget.

Consider these well-known "last words."

"Win one for the Gipper!"
—*George Gipp*

"I regret that I have but one life to give for my country."
—*Nathan Hale*

"Thomas Jefferson lives!"
—*John Adams*

Now that's the stuff. Or you could be memorably witty like these famous departees:

"I'm dying beyond my means."
—*Oscar Wilde*

"On the whole, I'd rather be in Philadelphia."
—*W.C. Fields*

"Always leave the shower curtain inside the tub!"
—*Conrad Hilton*

But whichever way you decide to say farewell, you need to do some advance planning. Otherwise, you're likely to leave the world with last words like:

"Oh shit!"
"Where's the bedpan?"
"Get me some new doctors!"
    or
"That nurse has great tits."

That would not be good. That would not be the way to cap off your wonderful and extraordinary life. Don't leave your last words to chance. Plan ahead. Come up with something that is:
1. Pithy
2. Moving or clever
3. Easily remembered
4. Not too long

If your final declaration is not carefully thought out you could wind up like Civil War General John Sedgwick who left the world with, "Don't worry. They're too far away. They couldn't hit an elephant at this dist..."

And remember that, once you've said your carefully planned last words, you should *shut up*. Otherwise, they won't be your last words!

But whatever you come up with, it probably won't be what those at your bedside really want you to say—which is—

"I'm leaving you all lots of money!"

ONE FINAL PIECE OF ADVICE

Having a fear of dying is certainly understandable—normal, perhaps. But some geezers have an *irrational* fear of the final adieu. There even exists, for a few, a fear of being buried alive. (George Washington, fearless in battle, suffered from this strange anxiety and instructed his family that he should not be buried for three days—just to make sure!) For this reason, several geezers, of recent, have asked to be buried with a *cell phone*. This is probably not a good idea. It would probably work out something like this:

(Geezer wakes up in a small enclosure, tries to sit up, bumps head, feels sides of enclosure, suddenly realizes he has been buried alive. Remembering his instructions to his family in such an event, he feels around for a cell phone. He finds it, picks it up, flips it open, punches the master button. It rings. . . and rings. . . and rings . . . Finally someone answers.)

Voice: "Welcome to the Premature Burial Hotline. This call may be monitored for quality assurance."
(Geezer in casket changes phone to other ear, face straining with concentration.)

Voice: "For English, press one. Para Español, numero dos. For any other language, press three and remain on the line."
(Geezer carefully presses a button.)

Voice: "Please listen carefully to the following options. The menu may have changed. If you are buried alive and would like someone to be notified, please select from the following. For your undertaker, press one. For your spouse, press two. For your doctor, press three. For your lawyer, press four."
(Geezer presses a button.)

Voice: "So that we may pass along all pertinent information, please select from the following: If you were buried yesterday, press one. If you were buried today, press two. If you have no idea when you were buried, press three.
(Geezer presses a button.)

Voice: "If you feel you are in good health, press one. If your health is slowly failing, press two. If you are near death, press three. If you have finally died, as you were supposed to do in the first place, don't press any buttons."
(Geezer feebly, and with great effort, manages to press yet another button.)

Voice: "The amount of remaining air in your casket will be a key factor in your successful retrieval. If you have enough air to survive for another day, press one. If you have enough air for only an hour or so, press two. If you feel your air is rapidly declining, press three."
(Geezer attempts to push another button, but fails.)

Voice: "Since you have not responded to any of these options, you are now being referred to one of our experienced and friendly associates. Please stay on the line."
(There is a lot clicking and humming. Geezer stirs slightly in his casket.)

Voice: "All of our associates are currently serving other customers. Please stay on the line. Your call is very important to us. Your call will be answered in the order in which it was received."
("Waiting music" is now heard—in this case, it is "Que Será, Será." The music plays...and plays...and then plays some more—geezer is now largely comatose.)

Voice: "All of our associates are busy with other callers. Please stay on the line. Your call is very ....

(Geezer, with one last conscious effort, begins stabbing wildly at the buttons.)

Voice: "We regret that option is not available. To return to the main menu, press one."

(Geezer revives just long enough to snap the cell phone shut. He then goes limp and gives up the ghost.)

"It must be his beeper."

"Will somebody pick a card, any card?"

CHAPTER SIXTEEN

A MODEST PROPOSAL
(For a Tribute to the World's Forgotten Geezers)

OVER THE CENTURIES, geezers, almost by definition, have outlived their contemporaries—and probably even outlasted most of their family members. So it can be assumed that many geezers have been put away with little ceremony, some even consigned to paupers' graves. Certainly many of their heirs were spared the expense of a headstone. Few—very few—led lives of such importance or grandeur that they are recalled by historians— or have had their names recorded in the world's archives.

And so, in memory of these long-forgotten geezers, we make the following modest proposal— in salute of their manifold contributions to the world's history of eccentricity and general, all-around grumpiness, a monument of their own...

THE TOMB OF THE UNKNOWN GEEZER

This magnificent edifice would be a dramatic reminder of what geezers down through the centuries have meant to mankind. It is suggested that a competition should be held among the world's leading architects to determine the precise design, although marble would be the absolutely necessary material to be used in its construction. It is further proposed that the tomb should be located in the Geezer National Park, whenever and wherever such a park is determined and designated by the Congress of the United States. In all probability this will not happen very soon.

"THE BACK PART OF THE BOOK"
(The part that no one ever reads!)

Including:
REFERENCES
SOURCES
FOOTNOTES
AND OTHER ADMISSIONS OF PLAGIARISM

At the back of most nonfiction books is a section intended to demonstrate how much effort and trouble the author went to in researching his book. No research of any kind went into this book, but, to follow tradition, the following sources are listed. They are entirely made up—like everything else in this book.

The Art of Grumpiness—by Sidney Scowl

How to Marry a Rich Old Geezer—by Anna Nicole Smith

Sex After 100—by I.M.A. Dreamer

How to Sue the Ass Off Almost Anyone—by Lee Tijus

Geezer Stats: Facts and Figures about the Senile and Insufferable—assembled by the Gnomes of Nantucket

The Success Secrets of Geezer CEOs—by The Business Squaretable

Wills, Bills and Chills: An Examination of the Geezer Lifestyle—by A. Sole

Lets Get Thrifty!—by Ebenezer Elderly

The Who's Who of Geezerhood—published by Marquis Publishers, London

It's Never Too Late to Hate—by Samuel Vitriol

How to Keep Your Driver's License In the Face of All Common Sense—by Hy Risk

The Geezer Mystique—by B.T. Frydenn

Geezer Wheels: The Guide to Proper Car Selection—published by the Automotive Review

Geezers Gone Wild!—the sequel to "Girls Gone Wild" (also available on DVD)

AND FINALLY WE COME TO. . .

THE END

(TWO WORDS THAT MOST GEEZERS
ARE LEAST ANXIOUS TO HEAR!)

"I told him it wouldn't kill him to try to be nice
once in a while, but I was wrong."

ABOUT THE AUTHOR

Charles F. "Chuck" Adams spent his career in international marketing and was President and Chief Operating Officer of D'Arcy, MacManus and Masius, Inc., one of the world's largest advertising agencies. Now retired, he continues to serve as Chairman of the Wajim Corporation and President of Adams Enterprises. He is also a former owner and General Partner of the Pittsburgh Penguins of the National Hockey League. He has chaired a number of charitable and civic organizations. He claims to be an avowed geezer.

BOOKS BY CHARLES F. ADAMS

Common Sense in Advertising
(McGraw-Hill, 1968)

Heroes of the Golden Gate
(Pacific Books, 1987)

California in the Year 2000
(Pacific Books, 1991)

The Magnificent Rogues
(Pacific Books, 1998)

Murder by the Bay
(Word Dancer Press, 2005)

The Complete Geezer Guidebook
(Quill Driver Books, 2009)